Keepin' It Real

First published in the UK in 2019 by
Intellect, The Mill, Parnall Road, Fishponds, Bristol, BS16 3JG, UK

First published in the USA in 2019 by
Intellect, The University of Chicago Press, 1427 E. 60th Street, Chicago, IL
60637, USA

A catalogue record for this book is available from the British Library.

Copy-editing: MPS Technology
Cover and Layout Design: Aleksandra Szumlas
Typesetting: Contentra
Production Manager: Tim Mitchell

Print ISBN: 978-1-78938-050-7
ePDF ISBN: 978-1-78938-052-1
ePUB ISBN: 978-1-78938-051-4

Printed & bound by Severn, Gloucester, UK.

To find out about all our publications, please visit
www.intellectbooks.com.
There, you can subscribe to our e-newsletter,
browse or download our current catalogue,
and buy any titles that are in print.

This is a peer-reviewed publication.

Keepin' It Real

Essays on Race
in Contemporary America

BY

Elwood David Watson

Bristol, UK / Chicago, USA

Contents

Introduction

It has been more than half a century since the late mid-twentieth-century Black intellectual renaissance author, and cultural critic, James Baldwin, wrote his classic, *The Fire Next Time* (Baldwin, 1963). Baldwin's work was riveting for its time. His spellbinding narrative examined the disturbing and vehement misunderstanding between Blacks (then Negroes) and Whites in regards to racial injustice of the era. His book became a catalyst for many progressive Americans of all racial groups, in that it prompted them into action and provided a passionate and eloquent voice for the modern civil rights movement. The book became a national bestseller and further catapulted him into the premier sphere of the American intellectual elite of all races. Today, as we move further into the twenty-first century, his prophetic message rings all too chillingly true.

It is a disappointing reality that many of the indignities (racial and otherwise), as well as differences in perceptions regarding the history and treatment of Black Americans ominously discussed during the 1960s, still apply today. This stark divide was evidenced in a poll conducted by CBS News in July 2015 that indicated 62 percent of all Americans (for Blacks the percentage was 68) believed that tensions in race relations were the highest they had been in twenty years (Sack & Thee-Brenan, 2015). Another poll taken in March of the same year by the Pew Research Center revealed similar attitudes (Pew Research Center, 2015). More telling was a poll taken by the same organization in August 2017, according to which, a sizable number of Americans across races indicated that they saw race relations to be fair at best and many interviewed saw them as poor. For Blacks, the percentage was 81 percent. For Whites, the number was 52 percent (Pew Research Center, 2017). It should come as little surprise that a disproportionate number of Black Americans have always been inclined to harbor more skeptical views on racial progress. History has given people of African descent good reason to embrace such cautionary views.

The circumstances of the past few years have certainly given any racially progressive person cause for pause: the attack on voting rights by many Southern states (Berman, 2015); the sinister targeting of many low-income and working-class Black home buyers by predatory lenders in the housing and financial industry (Loftin, 2010); the shocking initial indifference by many federal agencies, as well as the Bush administration, to the devastating impact that Hurricane Katrina had on its Black population in New Orleans in 2005 (Lavelle, 2006). We saw hope and despair on the faces of thousands of impoverished Black people of the city: men, women, children, and the elderly, which deeply demonstrated the racial and economic disenfranchisement rampant in the city. We have been witness to the horrendous treatment and disproportionate sentencing of Black people (especially Black men) in the criminal justice system (Alexander, 2010); the intense level of systematic and structural racism in our culture, as applicants with Black sounding names more likely to be discriminated against by potential employers than those with more "traditional" White-identified names (Bertrand & Mullainathan, 2003); massive defiance among many White radicals who vehemently and defiantly support the Confederate flag (Agiesta, 2015). White supremacists brazenly marched through Charlottesville and other American cities, feeling emboldened by the victory of Donald Trump and his racially divisive rhetoric in the 2016 election. The dilemma facing Black college graduates is that they are more than twice as likely to be unemployed as their White cohorts. Blacks, and in some cases, other non-White people, are profiled and harassed in various public and private venues. These are just a few examples of the current fractured racial climate (Jones & Schmitt, 2014).

The callous and disrespectful treatment of former President, Barack Obama, by his detractors was another major example of the current poisoned atmosphere (Capehart, 2015). Many Black Americans took Obama's mistreatment personally. They observed this blatant mistreatment of the president as a personal attack on themselves and the Black population in general (Facebook, 2015). The gullible assumption that America had become a post-racial society (if there can ever be such a thing as "post-racial") upon the election of President Obama was a radically misguided illusion.

As a Black college academic, I have had the privilege to converse over the past few years with fellow educated Black and non-Black professionals, some friends and others acquaintances. I have also investigated further, interacting through social media. I can personally attest that there currently exists an unmistakable level of paranoia, anger, in some cases fear, and most certainly resentment, to the current volatile situation that has gripped the nation. The temperature is hot and the climate has become dangerously unpredictable.

Prophetic Messages and Folk Heroes

Over a century ago, Black intellectual extraordinaire of his day, W. E. B. DuBois, stated that the problem of the twentieth century would be the problem of the color line (DuBois, 1903). This conclusion was shared, some forty years later (in 1944) by the renowned Swedish sociologist, Gunnar Myrdal, in *An American Dilemma: The Negro Problem and Modern Democracy* (Myrdal, 1944). Both were on target. Indeed, such a prophetic message is very relevant today in the twenty-first century. If the past several years have taught us anything, it is that the United States as a nation is in a perpetual state of crisis when it comes to the racial situation plaguing our nation. To put it bluntly, the past few years have left a brutal, brash, ugly stain of racism, sexism, homophobia, classism and xenophobia on America and other parts of the world touched by US society.

To be sure, our nation has seen worse times, given our often tumultuous history. Nonetheless, 2015, 2016, and 2017 may very well become three years for the record books. In fact, as far as recent history (post-1985) is concerned, not since 1994 can we remember a time that has been this racially, sexually, culturally, and religiously divisive (Watson, 2016).

From student unrest on college campuses to politicians openly espousing racist, sexist, xenophobic rhetoric; attacks on affirmative action; economic wealth gaps not seen since the Gilded Age; heightened racial tension; the proliferation of racial hate groups; the ongoing murders of unarmed Black, Brown, gay, lesbian, and transgendered people; violence against women, America has witnessed back-to-back years that have been anything but tranquil.

To refresh your memory, here are just some people and events that greeted us and made headlines over the past few years:

Donald Trump has confounded the pundits, critics and many others with his unexpectedly successful presidential campaign. Along the way, however, he has stoked the fires of jingoism, regressive populism, xenophobia, hatred, and other sorts of division with his irresponsible and racially coded language.

Rachel Dolezal, a former NAACP chapter president, caused much of the nation, particularly Black America, to gawk with disbelief once it was discovered that she was a biological White woman who passed herself off as Black for reasons that no one could quite understand. She had her supporters, many more detractors and dominated the news for several days.

Dylann Roof, the 21-year-old White supremacist, consumed by fear, personal insecurities, and racial hatred, betrayed the trust of bible study members at the Emanuel AME Church in Charleston, South Carolina, as he opened fire on them, killing nine parishioners. This horrific incident became known as the Charleston massacre. This senseless tragedy resulted in intense debates about the Confederate flag and culminated in the removal of the flag from the South Carolina State House.

Black Lives Matter protesters made their cause known as they disrupted the rallies of presidential candidates such as Vermont Sen. Bernie Sanders, Hillary Clinton, Jeb Bush and Donald Trump. With their bold, brash, fierce and no-apologies style, determined to shed light on the ongoing police violence that confronts far too many Black individuals and communities, the movement has managed to become a key player in the 2016 presidential campaign.

Jonathan Butler, a 25-year-old University of Missouri graduate student, and the Mizzou football team, were critical factors in the ultimate decision of former University of Missouri President, Timothy Wolfe, and university chancellor, R. Bowen Loftin, to resign from their posts. The campus had been roiled by protests from many Black students—bolstered by Butler's hunger strike and the team's planned boycott of games—who argued that

4

racism on the campus was a major problem. Similar protests were staged at Yale, Princeton, Vanderbilt and other institutions.

Colin Kaepernick, the NFL quarterback who made international headlines for his principled defiant stance in refusing to salute the American flag due to what he sees as the chronic injustices — social, cultural, legal, economic and more [...] plaguing Black and Hispanic people in America. His unapologetic activism managed to invoke the wrath of millions of Americans and endeared him to millions more.

#MeToo movement shed light on the sexual abuse and harassment of women across age groups. Whether it be athletes sexually violating women, high-level and powerful executives disrespecting and sexually abusing female colleagues and/or subordinates. The movement has prompted many women to respond to such injustices.

Violence against Black and Brown bodies. Numerous Black and some Hispanic citizens lose their lives at the hands of law enforcement. From Tamir Rice, Eric Garner, Michael Brown, Reika Boyd, Tanisha Anderson, LaQuan McDonald, Freddie Gray, Alton Shelton, Philando Castile, Korryn Gaines, Sandra Bland, and many others. In the case of 12-year-old Rice, he was shot by a police officer for having a toy gun in his pocket. Sandra Bland was found dead in her cell in Texas under mysterious circumstances. Eric Garner was choked to death by a police officer. LaQuan McDonald was shot seventeen times by a Chicago police officer. Freddie Gray was placed in the back of a police van and tied up, fracturing his spinal chord. In each of these cases, no one was indicted or held accountable for these deaths. A Texas grand jury refused to prosecute the officer in the Bland case, but the same officer was eventually indicted for perjury.

Targeting and harassing people of color. A number of non-White people have been targets of racial profiling and harassment by individual Whites, ranging from private citizens to law enforcement officers, for what these Whites see as an affront to their sensibilities or "invading their (Whites') space." This phenomenon has been described as "existing while Black" or "existing for not being White." Such incidents have been recorded with routine frequency and have prompted intense and passionate debate.

Other examples abound.

For many of us, our viewpoints on race have largely been formed by our personal experiences. In a nation that has been less than equitable to people of color, in particular, Black Americans, it is justifiable that many Black Americans are more inclined to believe that race is an intractable factor in our society that has an impervious grip on all people, regardless of race, either as perpetrators or oppressors. Many of us have stories of parents, grandparents, aunts, uncles, cousins, siblings, ourselves for that matter, who have been the recipients of its often poisonous venom. On the contrary, many Whites, particularly White men, are in positions where the specter of racial prejudice has little, if any, effect on their lives. Indeed, for many White males, institutional and structural racism is a vice of which they are largely, if not totally, immune.

The election of a Black president more than a decade ago notwithstanding, race is still the rambunctious, unruly elephant running wildly through the room. The feeling among many people across racial lines, particularly people of African descent, is that Black America is under unrelenting physical, psychological, and emotional siege.

This book explores several areas of race in the present era. Part I, "The Politics of Whitelash," discusses controversial events and volatile issues such as the Dylann Roof/Emanuel AME Church Massacre and the politics of White nationalism, the ugly specter of birtherism directed toward former President Obama, as well as the ongoing vile racial politics directed toward both Obama and his wife, Colin Kaepernick and the politics of White fragility, the nefarious racial politics that tinted the 2016 summer Olympics, and the rapid ascendancy of alt-right spokesmen and groups.

Part II, "Staying Woke!," examines controversial issues and debates that have perennially taken place within the Black community such as homophobia, misogyny, self-hatred, mental illness, and more recently, the rise of the Black Lives Matter movement, Black leaders being fair game for criticism, Black history month, reparations, and other related issues.

Part III, "Physical and Psychological Violence Against Black Bodies," explores past and present physical, psychological, and verbal assaults on Black and, in some cases, other non-White people. Topics such as Emmett Till, John Lewis, Sandra Bland, economic and political disenfranchisement, rampant police shootings, and the emotional impact that different forms of violence have had on segments of the Black community.

Part IV, "Soulful Reflections on Entertainment Icons and Celebrities," critiques a number of entertainers and events as they relate to Black

America, among them Bill Cosby, Jemele Hill, Donald Trump, Bill Maher, Aretha Franklin, Roseanne Barr, the derelict antics of some Black athletes, political pundits, and the often complex politics of popular culture.

Race is an entity that is frequently rife with controversy. It is an issue that is often blatant, intense, controversial, complex, confrontational, and frequently unpredictable. It is an undeniable factor that has firmly etched itself into the fabric of the American nation since its origins. The essays in this book confirm this reality.

REFERENCES

Agiesta, Jennifer (2015, July 2). Poll: Majority sees Confederate Flag as Southern pride symbol, not racist. *CNN Politics*. Retrieved from http://www.cnn.com/2015/07/02/politics/confederate-flag-poll-racism-southern-pride/

Alexander, Michelle (2010). *The new Jim Crow: Mass incarceration in the age of colorblindness*. New York, NY: The New Press.

Baldwin, James (1963). *The fire next time*. New York, NY: Dial Press.

Berman, Ari (2015, March 5). 50 years after Bloody Sunday, voting rights under attack. *The Nation*. Retrieved from http://www.thenation.com/article/50-years-after-bloody-sunday-voting-rights-are-under-attack/

Bertrand, Marianne, & Mullainathan, Sendhil (2004). Are Emily and Greg more employable than Lakisha and Jamal? A Field Experiment on Labor Market Discrimination. In S. Ferguson (Ed.), *Race, Gender, Sexuality and Class* (2nd ed., pp. 361–367). Thousand Oaks, California. Sage Publications.

Capehart, Jonathan (2015, March 6). Top 6 instances of disrespect toward President Obama. *The Washington Post*. Retrieved from http://www.washingtonpost.com/blogs/post-partisan/wp/2015/03/06/top-6-instances-of-disrespect-toward-president-obama/

Doherty, Carroll and Tyson, Alex (2015, May 4). Multiple views on Baltimore situation: Most say it was right decision to charge police officers. Retrieved from http://www.people-press.org/files/2015/05/5-4-2015-Baltimore-release.pdf

DuBois, W. E. B. (1903). *The souls of black folk*. Chicago, IL: AC McClurg & Company.

Jones, Janelle, & Schmitt, John (2014, May 27). A college degree is no guarantee. *National Journal*. Retrieved from http://cepr.net/publications/reports/a-college-degree-is-no-guarantee

Lavelle, Kristen (2006, July 1). Hurricane Katrina: The race and class debate. *The Monthly Review: An Independent Socialist Magazine, 58*(3). Retrieved from https://monthlyreview.org/2006/07/01/hurricane-katrina-the-race-and-class-debate/

Loftin, Britton (2010, October). Predatory lending targets minority neighborhoods. *Politics 365*. Retrieved from http://politic365.com/2010/10/07/predatory-lending-targeting-minority-neighborhoods/

Myrdal, Gunnar (1944). *An American dilemma: The Negro problem and modern democracy*. New York, NY: Harper & Bros.

Neal, Samantha (2017, August 29). Views of racism as a major problem increase sharply, especially among Democrats. *Pew Research Center*. Retrieved from http://www.pewresearch.org/fact-tank/2017/08/29/views-of-racism-as-a-major-problem-increase-sharply-especially-among-democrats

Stepler, Renee (2016, June 27). Social and demographic trends. *Pew Research Center*. Retrieved from http://www.pewresearch.org/fact-tank/2016/06/27/key-takeaways-race-and-inequality/

Sack, Kevin, & Thee-Brenan, Megan (2015, July 23). Poll finds most in U.S. hold dim view of race relations. *New York Times*. Retrieved from http://www.nytimes.com/2015/07/24/us/poll-shows-most-americans-think-race-relations-are-bad.html?_r=0

Thrush, Glenn, & Haberman, Maggie (2017, August 15). Trump gives White supremacists an unequivocal boost. *New York Times*. Retrieved from https://www.nytimes.com/2017/08/15/us/politics/trump-charlottesville-white-nationalists.html

Watson, Elwood (2016, January 19). 2015: Another challenging year for Black America. *Huffington Post*. Retrieved from https://www.huffingtonpost.com/elwood-d-watson/2015-another-challenging-_b_9016148.html?guccounter=1&guce_referrer_us=aHR0cHM6Ly91ay5zZWFyY2gueWWFob28uY29tLw&guce_referrer_cs=EyLWiDZZpkMtaT4kVrGiVA

PART I

The Politics of Whitelash

1

When Racism Hits Close to Home: On Your Campus

On September 28, 2016, a young White college student, Tristan John Rettke, then a freshman at East Tennessee State University, taunted a group of Black Lives Matter (BLM) supporters. He was bare-footed, dressed up as a gorilla, carrying a Confederate flag, taunting protesters with bananas, ropes, and nooses. He had a bag labeled "marijuana" and spoke in broken dialect. Rettke was immediately arrested (Tamburin, 2016) and eventually charged with civil rights intimidation in March 2017 (Campbell, 2017). When I first heard about the incident, I thought to myself, are we living in 2016 or 1916?!

From the United States to Norway to Kenya, Rettke's antics made both national and international news, through outlets as diverse as *USA Today* (Bowerman, 2016), *Washington Post* (Surluga, 2016), and *Inside Higher Education* (Saschick, 2016). As can be imagined, Black media — print, radio, television, and social media — got busy and wasted no time in taking this deranged fool to task about his arrogant, disrespectful, deplorable, and shamelessly racist behavior. Some of the criticism was downright woke (which is to say, enlightened and right on target) (Callahan, 2016).

As a professor who teaches at East Tennessee State University, I had an understandably curious and vested interest in what had gone down on my campus. What was even more interesting — and at the same time, disgusting — was that the incident took place at Borchuck Plaza. The plaza is only a few feet from my office at Rogers Stout Hall, which is located directly in front of the university library. Adding insult to injury, this is the plaza where a fountain was established to honor the five Black students — Eugene Caruthers, Elizabeth Watkins Crawford, Clarence McKinney,

11

George L. Nichol, and Mary Luellen Owens Wagner — who integrated the university in the 1950s. This is where the students were holding their protest.

As you can imagine, more than a little hell broke loose. Things went down much differently for the young, misguided soul who admitted that his intentions were to "provoke the Black protestors." Indeed, Retkke's antics became the stuff of global gossip. He became the latest poster boy for outlandish and shameful racism.

I was not on campus at the time of this disgusting display of subhuman behavior by Retkke and in some ways I am glad that I was not. Had I been, I might have been inclined to leave my office, run outside, confront him, and go all MBM (Mad Black Man) on his sorry butt. I am sure that is what many of the students he was taunting wanted to do as well.

That being said, I admire and commend our students involved in the peaceful protest for acting in just that manner, peacefully. They did not allow their emotions to overcome their better judgment. They did not sink or succumb to his pathetic level. Rather, they managed to let their message of peaceful and principled protest reign supreme.

Trust me, all of us who are well past our late teens (decades in my case), know that at that stage of your life, you can often react and snap, especially when you feel you are being disrespected and your humanity is being challenged. Again, bravo to the students at my institution!

Not surprisingly, certain factions on social media came to the defense of Rettke. Rather than acknowledge that he engaged in a behavior that was odious and deplorable, they decided to revert to intellectually dishonest comments and arguments denouncing Black Lives Matter as a hate group, that Blacks attack Whites all the time, and other nonsensical and indefensible blather.

The university administration was commended for its rapid response to the incident. ETSU President Brian Noland released a thoughtful statement to the ETSU Student Body and the larger ETSU community, in which he praised the BLM student protesters for handling a situation that could have ended up with a very ugly and volatile outcome with grace and dignity. Later that evening, there was public forum at the University Culp Center, where a number of faculty, administrators, and students attended to express their thoughts on the event and their feelings about the overall climate as it related to race relations on campus. As I see, East Tennessee State University is like most campuses. To be sure, given the institutions history, there is significant room for improvement.

The following day, another professor and I started off a class we were co-teaching that semester by discussing the incident, before moving onto the subject that was scheduled for discussion. As it turned out, several of the students in the course had actually participated in the protest. The discussion was indeed lively at times.

As earlier stated, I did not arrive at the campus until later in the afternoon on the day of the incident and was not aware of it until one of my colleagues, who happens to be White, came to my office and told me about it. It was clear that he was visibly perplexed.

Upon hearing the news, I was shocked. Not at the fact that a student harbored racist beliefs or attitudes, but rather, what surprised me was the level of disrespectful behavior this guy engaged in. One can only speculate as to whether they will conduct a psychological evaluation on this young man.

Rettke was/is a very callous, arrogant, and disgracefully racist human being. He obviously has little, if any regard, for the human dignity of other people who are different from him. It is a sad commentary for sure. Nonetheless, in spite of the shameless behavior he exhibited, justice did prevail and the results will likely follow him for quite some time, and possibly forever.

REFERENCES

Bowerman, Mary (2016, September 29). Student arrested after wearing gorilla mask to Black Lives Matter protest. *USA Today*. Retrieved from https://eu.usa-today.com/story/news/nation-now/2016/09/29/student-arrested-after-wearing-gorilla-mask-black-lives-matter-protest/91259986/

Callahan, Yesha (2016, September 29). White student in gorilla mask taunts Black Lives Matter at East Tennessee State University. Retrieved from theroot.com/grapevine

Campbell, Becky (2017, March 21). Former ETSU student indicted on civil rights intimidation, disorderly conduct charges. *Johnson City Press*. Retrieved from https://www.johnsoncitypress.com/Courts/2017/03/21/Former-ETSU-student-indicted-on-civil-rights-intimidation-disorderly-conduct-charges

Jaschick, Scott (2016, September 30). Ugly response to Black Lives Matter. *Inside Higher Education*. Retrieved from https://www.insidehighered.com/news/2016/09/30/east-tennessee-state-shaken-when-black-lives-matter-event-disrupted

Surluga, Susan (2016, September 29). Student arrested after wearing gorilla mask, handing out bananas at Black Lives Matter protest. *The Washington Post*. Retrieved from https://www.washingtonpost.com/news/grade-point/wp/2016/09/29/student-arrested-after-wearing-gorilla-mask-handing-out-bananas-at-black-lives-matter-protest/?noredirect=on&utm_term=.e254b4f9b11c

Tamburin, Adam (2016 September 29). Tennessee student arrested after wearing gorilla mask to Black Lives Matter protest. *Tennessean*. Retrieved from https://eu.tennessean.com/story/news/education/2016/09/29/etsu-student-arrested-after-wearing-gorilla-mask-black-lives-matter-protest/91268320/

2

The 2016 Olympics: The Trilogy of Hypocrisy, Racism, and White Privilege

The 2016 Rio Summer Olympics was an event packed with suspense, intrigue, and drama. Anticipation about the games had been intense even before the competition began. One thing can be said for certain, the athletic competition did not disappoint as there was hardly a dull moment.

The US Women's gymnastics and swimming teams made many Americans proud with their overwhelming domination at the games. Millions of Americans of all races, religions, ethnic groups, and sexual orientations cheered as Simone Biles, Gabby Douglas, Laurie Hernandez, Michelle Carter, Claressa Shields, Brianna Rollins, Simone Manuel, and other women of color broke records and performed admirably with classic and powerful precision. Fellow gymnast Aly Raisman demonstrated formidable skill as she managed to secure a number of silver medals. It was a glorious sight to witness.

Unfortunately, there was another more disturbing element that overshadowed (some argued dominated) the 2016 Olympic games: racism (Moorehead, 2016). Yes, race reared its perverse and divisive attitude and occasionally saturated the often positive spirit of the games. NBA great LeBron James received racial backlash and criticism for his loving shout-outs to Simone Biles and Simone Manuel, praising them for their masterful performances. LeBron was taken to task by many bloggers chastising him for supposedly "making" race an issue (Callahan, 2016).

Gabby Douglas was continually attacked for her hairstyle choices (really, is it about her hair!?) as well as seemingly failing to place her hand over her heart and smile during the playing of the national anthem. Track-and-field gold medalist Rollins was called out for having the "audacity" (sarcasm) to proudly state that "Black Girls Rock" after winning her competition.

On the other hand, numerous Internet users (mostly White men) were making outlandish excuses for the behavior of US swimmer Ryan Lochte and his band of swimmers who from all recent evidence and news reports apparently lied about being pulled over and robbed at gunpoint in Rio. The three other swimmers were detained by Brazilian authorities. For the record, Lochte did issue a tepid, if not forthright, apology (Romero, 2016).

What was ironic, although not all that surprising for anyone who is attuned to racial politics particularly as they relate to the history of American race relations, is the fact that many of these critics who attacked LeBron James for his support of two fellow African-Americans had no problem in making ridiculous (one could argue pathetic) excuses for Lochte, who was simultaneously dropped by several major corporate sponsors, and the inexcusable antics of his fellow swimmers — Gunnar Bentz, Jack Conger, and Jimmy Feigen. Such defenses ranged from "they were just having fun," "they just got caught up in the moment," "boys will be boys," (Lochte was 32 years old at the time and all the other men were in their late 20s/early 30s) to the, unbelievable, "I can understand why they did what they did," and so on (Abad-Santos, 2016).

One can only imagine what the outcry would be if a group of Black athletes had gotten drunk, fabricated a story about being held up, lied to the police, and had their hoax uncovered. Social media would have been filled with phony self-righteous indignation demanding that the athletes in question forfeit their medals as well as the other almost certain hostile racial commentary that would follow (Cave, 2016).

On the contrary, many of the same apologists viciously attacked Gabby Douglas. She was raked over the coals, called every disrespectful name under the sun, and had her character assassinated in the court of public opinion. It was a disgraceful, racial double standard. Indeed, it was the intersection of White arrogance and privilege at its most perverse (Jensen, 2016).

There were those who argued that Ryan Lochte was not White. Well guess what? Despite the debate that engulfed some quarters about Lochte's Cuban American background versus White, etc., he identifies as White and there are many Hispanics who are White. One thing is for certain: the media had/ has certainly classified him and awarded him White male status.

The more insulting, in fact hypocritical, factor that has arisen from this situation is that many of these same commentators who have targeted fellow bloggers who dare invoke racial solidarity and pride in their praise of fellow Black athletes are the same people who, more than often, look at life through a sharply impermeable racial prism. The truth is, whether they are willing to acknowledge or deny this hard truth, a large number of people, in particular, White people, do indeed make many decisions that are based on race:

- Where to live
- Who to marry
- Who to be friends with
- Where to send their kids to school
- Who to hire for more desired types of jobs
- Where to worship
- Who to do business with
- What politicians to support or vote for (most of the time)

and so on.

While many of these same, supposedly color blind, racially liberated folks may see themselves as such, the truth is that they are often anything but. To these men and women, race does indeed matter. Such intellectual dishonesty personifies the height of hypocrisy. Racism, double standards, White denial, and racial resistance are real facts of everyday life. However, for most people of color, we did not need the 2016 Olympic Games to shed light on such a grim reality.

REFERENCES

Abad-Santos, Alex (2016, August 15). Rio 2016: Gabby Douglas Olympics experience fits the pattern of how we treat black female athletes. *Vox*. Retrieved from https://www.vox.com/2016/8/15/12476322/gabby-douglas-rio-olympics-racism

Callahan, Yesha (2016, August 17). LeBron James upsets white fans after praising black Olympic athletes. *The Root*. Retrieved from https://thegrapevine.theroot.com/lebron-james-upsets-white-fans-after-praising-black-oly-1790888844

Cave, Damien (2016, August 12). Race and the Olympic games. *New York Times*. Retrieved from https://www.nytimes.com/2016/08/12/us/race-related-rio-2016-olympic-games.html

Jensen, Emily (2016, August 24). Rio 2016 proved that racism and sexism are still very much our problem. *Paste*. Retrieved from https://www.pastemagazine.com/articles/2016/08/rio-2016-proved-that-racism-and-sexism-are-still-v.html

Moorehead, Monica (2016, September 1). Racism, sexism tarnish Olympic games. *Munda Abrevo Workers World*. Retrieved from https://www.workers.org/2016/09/01/racism-sexism-tarnish-olympic-games/

Romero, Simon (2016, August 19). Ryan Lochte apologizes "for my behavior" after his robbery claim. *New York Times*. Retrieved from https://www.nytimes.com/2016/08/20/sports/olympics/ryan-lochte-apology-rio-olympics.html

3

Dylann Storm Roof: The Deranged, Dark Face of White Nationalism

Imagine the scenario. You invite a person, in fact a stranger, into your home at their request. On the surface he seems to be normal, sincere, and interested in getting to know you better and being a part of your life and community. Everything seems to be going smoothly. Suddenly, out of nowhere, the individual you have befriended suddenly pulls out a gun and decides to murder you and your fellow family, friends, and associates. Almost unimaginable, right? This was the horrifying scenario that took place at the Emmanuel AME Church in Charleston, South Carolina, on June 17, 2015.

This is the house of worship where mass murderer Dylann Storm Roof betrayed the kindness and generosity of the members who granted him permission to worship in fellowship and communion with them. After sitting quietly in a church pew for over an hour, Roof suddenly jumps up, makes the misguided and deluded charge that Black men are raping White women and that Black people are abusing and taking over America and must be violently stopped from doing so.

He then proceeds to gun down various church members, eventually taking the lives of nine men and women. Three of his victims were over 70 years old, including an 87-year-old great-grandmother. The church pastor and state senator Clementa C. Pinckney was also a victim of this madness. Roof decided to spare the life of one church attendee, informing her that he wanted her to tell the world what had transpired. Murdering people in church: incomprehensible.

Needless to say, Roof's action left the congregation members and the nation perplexed, stunned, and outraged at such a sadistic act of homeland terrorism. Roof, at the time, was a 21-year-old White male with White supremacist affinities and ties. He had a history of deviant behavior and drug use. The sad and sobering truth is that this was hardly the first time that a Black church had been the target of homegrown terrorism by White supremacists.

Attacks on Black churches have been a common occurrence in America since the nation's inception. The ongoing and relentless bombing and burning of churches during the era of the modern civil rights movement of the 1950 and 1960s, as well as the intense period of church burnings that occurred in the South and in pockets of the Midwest during the mid-1990s, were indicative of a long and tormented history of violence directed toward Black houses of worship and Black Christianity in general.

Black ministers, such as the late Rev. Fred Shuttlesworth and Dr. Martin Luther King Jr., were under relentless attack from the Ku Klux Klan, other virulent and vicious racists, and, in some cases, Southern law enforcement. In the case of Dr. King, he managed to earn the deep enmity of then-FBI director J. Edgar Hoover and the FBI in general. The hostility directed toward these men also placed their welfare and that of those close to them in jeopardy. The behavior of Dylann Storm Roof, who had conveyed his intention to start a race war, was an act of racial terrorism. Pure and simple (McLaughlin, 2015).

There were media outlets that were reluctant to ascribe this label to Roof and, rather, decided to focus on the fact that he was vulnerable to mental illness. This is a disturbing example of intellectual dishonesty. The fact is that there are many people who suffer from mental illness, yet do not go on mass murder sprees and deviously plot to kill other human beings.

This was a premeditated attack. He purposely targeted a church with Black parishioners to inflict his acts of racialized violence upon its members. Dylann Storm Roof is a bigot and his actions were driven by hardcore bigotry. His deeds and actions have made this evident. There is no other way to describe it (Bever, 2017).

After details of the tragic event became known, a number of White nationalists/supremacists attempted to distance themselves from Roof and declared him as an "outlier," an aberration, a mentally unstable social deviant, and so forth, citing examples of his past behavior (Nobles and Stewart, 2015). Numerous race-oriented websites saw a number of its subscribers express considerable concern that Roof's actions would make it considerably more difficult for such groups to successfully recruit new members and that current membership would, in fact, decline. Donald Trump's presidential victory, a year later in November 2016, quickly put such concerns to rest. Trump's win was a boon to White nationalism and they eagerly embraced him as someone who was significant to their agenda. Truth be told, given the long history of racial paranoia among many fringe segments of American society, such a prospect should not have been all that surprising.

Racial hostility notwithstanding, Roof's atrocious act of violent racism was likely the catalyst for prompting then South Carolina governor Nikki Haley in conjunction with several other prominent South Carolina politicians includ- ing Jim Clyburn, Tim Scott, Lindsey Graham, Mark Sanford, and others to hold a press conference on June 22, 2015 denouncing the act of having the confederate flag flying above the statehouse in Columbia and advocating its removal from the capital grounds (Shoichet, Fentz, and Yan, 2015).

Needless to say, such a move did not win Haley, Scott, Graham, Sanford, or many other southern politicians throughout the region the support of many White southerners. Rather, taking such a position caused them to earn the widespread wrath of many voters, particularly those voters who saw these politicians as pandering to political correctness. Nonetheless, Governor Hale and her fellow politicians took the political high road and morally correct position. Such a principled stance is to be commended.

What was even more indescribably inspiring was witnessing numerous family members of the victims of Roof's madness confront such a madman and tell him that they forgave him for his behavior. Millions of people both in America and throughout the entire world were in awe of such Christian behavior. It is probably safe to say that most people who consider themselves relatively forgiving human beings came to the realization that most of us, no matter our level of Judeo/Christian behavior, had/have not reached such an admirable level of growth and maturity. The actions of these men and women served as a phenomenal example for all of us to adhere to. Forgive- ness aside, a grand jury did find Dylann Roof guilty in January 2017 and he was given the death penalty (Jarvie, 2017).

While the nation has made considerable strides, the fact is that racism is still a potent adversarial force in the lives of far too many Black Americans. This is evident in chronically high unemployment rates in many Black (and Brown) communities and obscenely high incarceration among Black men. Rampant police brutality has also affected and demoralized too many Black communities. Black college graduates are more than twice as likely to be unemployed or underemployed as their White counterparts. Unprecedented levels of gentrification have and continue to displace disproportionate numbers of Black working-class and lower-income people. There is still work to be done.

It will take a long time, if ever, for the residents of Charleston, South Carolina, the family of the victims, and perhaps even members of Roof's family to fully heal from such a senseless tragedy. The fact that many of his victims were able to confront this vicious racist monster, look him in the eye, and sincerely tell him that they were able to grant him their forgiveness is both remarkable and astounding (Coates, 2016). They are true, genuine, and dedicated Christians. The same is true of the many citizens across racial groups who demonstrated their support and solidarity and took a stand against such vehement and violent racial hatred.

In the meantime, Dylann Roof aside, what we can do is make a genuine effort to come to grips with the fragmentation plaguing our nation and make a valiant effort to rectify and heal such an unhealthy level of potentially destructive economic, racial, religious, political, and cultural stratification.

REFERENCES

Bever, Lindsey (2017, May 17). "I'm just a sociopath" Dylan Roof declared after deadly church shooting rampage, Court records say. *The Washington Post.* Retrieved from https://www.washingtonpost.com/news/post-nation/wp/2017/05/17/im-just-a-sociopath-dylann-roof-declared-after-deadly-church-shooting-spree-court-records-say/?utm_term=.6f5574c4655c

Coates, Ta-Nehishi (2016, May 26). Killing Dylan Roof. *The Atlantic.* Retrieved from https://www.theatlantic.com/politics/archive/2016/05/dylann-roof-death-penalty/484274/

Jarvie, Jenny (2017, January 10). Jury condemns Dylann Roof to death for Charleston S.C., Church shooting that killed nine. *Los Angeles Times.* Retrieved from https://www.latimes.com/nation/la-na-charleston-roof-sentencing-20170110-story.html

McLaughlin, Michael (2015, June 20). Racist manifesto purportedly written by Dylan Roof surfaces online. *Huffington Post.* Retrieved from https://www.huffingtonpost.co.uk/entry/dylann-roof-manifesto-charleston-shooting_n_7627788

Nobles, Frances, & Stewart, Nikita (2015, July 16). Dylan Roof's past reveals trouble at home and school. *New York Times.* Retrieved from https://www.nytimes.com/2015/07/17/us/charleston-shooting-dylann-roof-troubled-past.html

Shoichet, Catherine E., Fentz, Ashley, & Yan, Holly (2015, June 22). Charleston: Governor, Senator join in saying flag should go. *The Muslim Times.* Retrieved from https://themuslimtimes.info/2015/06/22/charleston-governor-senators-join-in-saying-confederate-flag-should-go/

4

Conservatives Still Scapegoating Barack Obama

Throughout their eight years in the White house, many Republican politicians, pundits, and loyal GOP voters targeted former President Obama (and, in some cases, former First Lady Michelle Obama) as the reason for the current state of race relations in the United States. As those in the land of rock-ribbed Republicanism saw it, our former U.S. commander-in-chief was/is the primary reason that the racial situation is less than desirable.

From former FOX News host and 2016 presidential candidate Mike Huckabee to retired neurosurgeon (also 2016 presidential candidate) Ben Carson, to Louisiana governor, another 2016 candidate, Bobby Jindal, to the always flame-throwing, fire in the mouth, tea party darling, and also 2016 candidate Ted Cruz — each of these conservative Republican politicians laid the downturn in racial harmony squarely at the feet of the president. Needless to say, they were not alone. Even some mainstream media commentators weighed in on the issue (Cafferty, 2011).

Right-wing talk radio has made blaming President Obama for race relations a cottage industry. In fact, I had not seen anyone blamed so much for a situation since former Bush administration official Michael Brown was scapegoated for the ineffectiveness of FEMA during the hurricane Katrina tragedy in 2005. Perennial Obama critics Rush Limbaugh and Sean Hannity; acid-tongued author and commentator Ann Coulter; outlandish radical Obama haters Mark Levin and Alex Jones; sophisticated Obama critic Erik Erickson; and Hugh Hewitt, Ben Ferguson, and others have made criticizing the former president for racial strife a sporadic affair. In fact, among the right-wing punditry, criticizing President Obama had/has become an obsessive, "round the clock hobby for a large segment of these individuals" (Cooper, 2016).

Race relations did not worsen under President Obama, however. They are indeed less than desirable and far from ideal, but the fact is that it has always been the case. From the time African slaves were bought ashore and stepped foot on American soil to the present day, race relations between different ethnic groups has always been complex and complicated at best.

America has always had a tortured racial past. Neither has the nation's gender history been much better. From slavery to the Civil War and from the reactionary 1980s to the twenty-first century, race (like gender) is an ongoing topic that has been deeply etched into the fabric of a conflicted and unsettled nation. This is nothing new (Coates, 2017).

Rather, what transpired was that, during his tenure in office, largely due to his race, many people were forced to confront the issue of race as well as their own racism. Sad as it is, the truth is that the fact that a man of African descent was the leader of the free world was too much for many of these people to bear (Dyson, 2017). To these people the Obama presidency is the equivalent of having a bad nightmare from which they had not yet awakened.

The "blame Obama" message was on full display in August 2017 when President Trump, along with other right-wing activists, attempted to put the blame on President Obama for the unrest that occurred between White supremacists and Antifa activists in Charlottesville, Virginia, indicating that this unrest was the result of the sentiment that had been cultivated by the previous occupant in the White House (Stein, 2017). As can be imagined, hell broke loose as many people took to Facebook, Twitter, Instagram, various other forms of social media, and to the op-ed pages of major newspapers to express their outrage at those attempting to scapegoat the former president (Dyson, 2017).

President Trump has always seemed to be in some sort of entangle-ment with his predecessor. From the moment Obama officially entered the White House in 2009, during his tenure as president, and even after he had left the White House in January 2017, Trump had/has been obsessed with Barack Obama. He has mercilessly attacked him on Twitter and other public forums (Fabian, 2017), and he seems to be all too eager to deconstruct the Obama legacy.

For many bigots, Black leaders of state are supposed to be relegated to literary fiction or to the imaginary creative spaces of Hollywood portrayed by actors such as James Earl Jones, Morgan Freeman, and Chris Rock. It is these sorts of fictionalized accounts of Black presidencies where such limited idealism is supposed to end. Psychologically speaking, this is where many of the president's critics dwell in terms of emotion and values (Dyson, 2017).

Let's keep it real here. As a historian, I can tell you with unalloyed confidence that neither President Obama nor his wife is responsible for the more than 400 years of racial strife that has plagued this nation from its inception. He and his administration did not pull Union troops out of the South and end Reconstruction in the mid- to late-nineteenth century (that was Rutherford B. Hayes and his vice president, Samuel Tilden), which led to the demise of the brief Black political enfranchisement in the South and other regions of the United States. It allowed the South to return to its previous behavior of terrorizing, oppressing, and demoralizing Black citizens through the sadistic employment of Jim Crow laws, grandfather clauses, colored (yes, "colored," that was the term used at the time) and White water fountains, poll taxes, literacy tests, and, in a number of cases, lynchings and other forms of physical violence.

Such vicious forms of political, social, emotional, economic, and psychological denigration and degradation manifested themselves in the culture of the South for more than a half century right up until the mid-twentieth century long before our current president was born or held political office. President Obama can plead not guilty.

Does this mean that the president is devoid of any responsibility in regards to race? Of course not. There are a number of people (I am one of them) who have at times felt that the president has not taken an aggressive enough stance on discussing racial issues. In some cases, we feel that he has erred on the side of caution far too often in an effort to placate, pacify, or, at the very least, neutralize his critics who monitor every comment he makes and were/are ready to pounce on or, in many cases, distort comments he makes in regards to race.

That being said, I can also understand why he was and still is often apprehensive in public about really engaging in any sort of racial discussion for this very reason. The tender feelings of some on the conservative right (and some faux liberals) can be easily offended by people of color and other anti-racist activists who candidly and unabashedly speak truth to power. White fragility is a long embedded nuisance in our culture.

The cold, hard fact is that race has been, is, and, for the foreseeable future, will be a crucial and ongoing issue for Americans of all political, racial, and cultural backgrounds to deal with, long after President Obama, President Trump, those of you reading this piece, myself, and others have departed from this earth. Therefore, it is best that we decide to approach the subject aggressively, deftly, practically, and wisely during our individual lifetimes.

REFERENCES

Cafferty, Jack (2011, September 11). Has President Obama made racism worse? *CNN*. Retrieved from http://caffertyfile.blogs.cnn.com/2011/09/27/has-president-obama-made-racism-worse/.

Coates, Ta-Nehisi (2017). *We were eight years in power: An American tragedy.* Chino Valley, AZ: One World Press.

Cooper, Clint (2016, July 24). Obama's lack of race-blind leadership worsens race relations. *Times Free Press*. Retrieved from https://www.timesfreepress.com/news/opinion/freepress/story/2016/jul/24/cooper-post-racial-misapplication/377146/

Dyson, Michael (2017). *Tears we cannot stop: A sermon to White America.* New York, NY: St. Martin's Press.

Dyson, Michael Eric (2017, August 18). Is Obama to blame for Trump — and the revival of white supremacists here? *Washington Post*. Retrieved from https://www.washingtonpost.com/outlook/is-obama-to-blame-for-trump--and-the-revival-of-white-supremacist-hate/2017/08/17/f0939fbe-836f-11e7-b359-15a3617c767b_story.html?utm_term=.4d161ef249b0

Fabian, Jordan (2017, April 6). Trump feud with Obama intensifies. *The Hill*. Retrieved from https://thehill.com/homenews/administration/327529-trump-feud-with-obama-intensifies

Stein, Jeff (2017, August 15). Barack Obama is to blame. 13 Alabama conservatives on Charlottesville. *Vox*. Retrieved from https://www.vox.com/policy-and-politics/2017/8/15/16148144/alabama-conservatives-on-charlottesville

5

Colin Kaepernick: The Undeniable Reality of American Racial Hypocrisy

No one can deny that the Colin Kaepernick/American flag saga has kept more than a few people talking. Indeed, millions of Americans from varied walks of life and across political and economic lines have not been hesitant to weigh in on the most recent high-profile drama to rock professional football.

As most people already know, Kaepernick sparked a major firestorm when he refused to stand during the playing of the national anthem. His primary reason for the protest was his unyielding belief that American society has failed to live up to the principles that it espouses in the Constitution. To put it more bluntly, Kaepernick views (accurately) America as a nation that frequently mistreats and abuses its Black and other non-White citizens.

As one can imagine, reaction was swift. The usual major forces of social media, Facebook and Twitter, nosedived into excessive commentary, much of it highly critical of Kaepernick. Comments ranged from "ungrateful," "unpatriotic," "mulatto" (referring to the fact that Kaepernick is biracial), "incompetent," and "worthless" to disgraceful expletives. Not surprisingly, much of the criticism directed toward Kaepernick came from Whites, many of whom were not above engaging in racial slurs and other forms of racial invective.

It is also important to note that there were some Black folk who jumped on the "Kaepernick is out of line" bandwagon. Jerry Rice, Tiki Barber, Rodney Harrison (who questioned Kaepernick's Blackness), Stephen A. Smith (who said, "We Black people must start looking in the mirror"), Jason Whitlock, and others took the pro football player to task for what they saw as misguided behavior and actions. Whitlock's mean-spirited attacks on Kaepernick understandably drew outrage from many people across racial lines (Masisak, 2017).

Back to Harrison and others who share his misguided view for a moment. It always perplexes and, in fact, disturbs me when certain fellow Black folk decide to wallow and sit in judgment of another person's Black bonafides. This was the same "he is not an authentic brother" venom that was directed toward *Grey's Anatomy* actor Jessie Williams following his impassioned speech at the 2015 BET Awards.

What these critics of men and women like Kaepernick and Williams fail to realize or tend to forget is the fact that many leaders of the Black community from Frederick Douglass, Booker T. Washington, Sojourner Truth, W. E. B. DuBois, Walter White (hell, Barack Obama for that matter), and many others were/are biracial Black people. While they (to some extent) may have been afforded certain advantages that other Black people of their respective eras were denied, they still were largely viewed and treated as colored people (the term used to refer to Black people of that time period) by the larger society and they saw themselves as such. They had the respect of segments of the White power structure of the day and utilized their influence to make change for the larger community. They realized that White racists, systematic and systemic racism, and racial oppression did not discriminate when it came to Black folk, including themselves.

The majority of Whites who threw shade on Kaepernick did so from old-fashioned racist rhetoric. These were the White men (and some women) who saw him as uppity, ungrateful, unpatriotic, and some even referred to him as "ugly" and arrogant. Constant references have been made about Kaepernick's multi-millionaire status and his supposed "ungratefulness" to all the fans (read, White people) and the nation that have made his financial situation possible. This was a common theme in the many acerbic comments that have permeated social media. The message was that Kaepernick should shut up, know his place, and play ball (Watson, 2016).

The not so subtle (in fact, blatantly racist) and profoundly arrogant and ignorant argument being made here is that Black Americans are not legitimate citizens of America and that our very existence is supposed to be periodically reviewed and verified by others. Please! Guess what? The 14th amendment settled this question once and for all in 1868. Signed, sealed, and delivered!

Telling Black people that we cannot express our constitutionally given rights only confirms the incorrect assumption that we have no rights.

We can, dance, sing, play ball and entertain White people in all manner of fashion. This is allowed and is to be lauded. However, once we take a stand and call out any or varied injustices that are routinely perpetrated on people of African descent we have supposedly stepped out of bounds and forgotten our supposed places of racial submission. Such racial paternalism is abhorrent.

Kaepernick has garnered the support of many people including fellow athletes, a number of military veterans, and politicians and legendary entertainers such as Georgia congressman John Lewis, Harry Belafonte, and others. He joins a distinguished, select list of Black Americans who fell out of favor with White society when they embraced heroic principles over political, social, and economic comfort. Such a distinguished membership includes Paul Robeson, Muhammad Ali, Fannie Lou Hamer, Fred Shuttlesworth, and many, many others. Such men and women are to be commended for their courage and commitment to justice.

It is very troubling and telling that many of these same individuals who would deny Kaepernick the right to utilize his first amendment rights are the very people who have no apprehension engaging and exercising their constitutional rights no matter how vile, unprofessional, racist, or disrespectful (Bianco, 2016). Moreover, many of them are the same people who have enthusiastically cheered when Donald Trump engages in vicious diatribes in his criticisms of America and others who have earned his frequent wrath. It was/is evident that these people see dissent and free speech as reserved for Whites only. In essence, free speech for me, but not for thee (Grigo, 2017).

As of this moment, in 2018, Kaepernick is still a free agent as no team has signed him. The obscene level of hypocrisy is staggering. The fact is that many of these so-called patriotic Americans have been so adamant in their efforts to vilify Colin Kaepernick for taking the position he has that they have failed miserably in their efforts to even listen to or consider his position. Rather, they have dismissed him as an entity unworthy of humanity (Moorehead, 2016).

Racism is a factor in American society that is as old as the republic itself. It is deeply embedded in the DNA of our culture. The unjust level of vitriol directed toward Colin Kaepernick demonstrated this fact all too well. Such attitudes personify classic examples of White supremacy, White fragility, and White privilege.

REFERENCES

Bianco, Marcie (2016, September 2). Colin Kaepernick's protest highlights America's racist hypocritical attitude toward patriotism. *Quartz*. Retrieved from https://qz.com/772541/colin-kaepernicks-protest-highlights-americas-racist-hypocritical-attitude-toward-patriotism/

Editorial Board (2017, August 7). Kaepernick wasn't the issue in Dolphins Q.B. search: It was our hypocrisy on race. *Miami Herald*. Retrieved from https://www.miamiherald.com/opinion/editorials/article165966412.html

Masisak, Corey (2017, September 6). Jason Whitlock finds new low in crusade against Kaepernick. *New York Post*. Retrieved from https://nypost.com/2017/09/06/jason-whitlock-finds-new-low-in-crusade-against-kaepernick/

Moorehead, Monica (2016, September 11). Colin Kaepernick's political rebellion exposes US reality. *Truthout*. Retrieved from https://truthout.org/articles/colin-kaepernick-s-political-rebellion-exposes-us-reality/

Rafeedie, Matthew (2016, September 13). The hypocrisy of many Kaepernick critics. *Odyssey*. Retrieved from https://www.theodysseyonline.com/the-hypocrisy-of-many-kaepernick-critics

Watson, Elwood (2016, September 13). Colin Kaepernick and the politics of race, arrogance and hypocrisy. *The Good Men Project*. Retrieved from https://goodmenproject.com/featured-content/colin-kaepernick-and-the-politics-of-race-arrogance-and-hypocrisy-wcz/

6

Birtherism = Bullshit

On September 16, 2016 at a televised press conference, Donald Trump finally admitted what the rational and sane among us always had known. He conceded that President Obama was born in the United States and was thus a legitimate American citizen. This latent and belated admission by the 2016 GOP nominee supposedly closed the long-running and rambling chapter that had been written over the past few years (Smith and Tau, 2011). All previous denunciations and skepticism by Trump came to an abrupt halt, in theory, on this date (Glass, 2016).

Like many, if not virtually everything that involves Trump, the admission was not without controversy. Rather than admit that he had engaged in a perverse level of irresponsible behavior, he shifted the blame to his presidential rival Hillary Clinton and her campaign staffs — both past and present — for creating such a foul rumor (Edrorgo, 2016). Clinton quickly and effectively refuted any allegations that her campaign had anything to do with such sinister antics and denounced Trump as being disgraceful. The mainstream media immediately supported Clinton's claim that neither she nor her campaign was involved with the "President Obama is not an American birther nonsense" (Rees, 2016).

Speaking of the mainstream media, anyone who followed that story at the time could witness the intense level of anger, annoyance, disgust, and resentment that was reverberating on many news networks. It was clear that many reporters, news anchors, radio hosts, and other media folk felt a sharp pain in their gut as if they had been kicked in the stomach. It was the feeling that many people get once they come to the realization that they had been conned. It was obvious that segments of the press were wiping egg off their faces and many were sucking their thumbs both publicly and privately. CNN anchor John King bluntly stated, "It looks like we have been played." His assessment was spot on.

President Trump had manipulated the media by insinuating he had blockbusting information regarding President Obama's birth. Instead, he made the comment that Obama was in fact born in the United States. In the end, Trump gained free publicity for the opening of his brand new hotel, where many journalists had booked rooms overnight in anticipation of big news that ultimately turned out to be a dud.

The fact is that large portions of the media contributed to the Trump juggernaut/phenomenon. Almost immediately since announcing his campaign for president, Trump was afforded nonstop press and in some cases preferential treatment that was largely absent for other presidential candidates in the form of scheduling, espousing rhetoric, and making statements that bordered on the ridiculous. Thus, the result of the September 2016 press conference was a classic example of chickens coming home to roost.

Once Trump had finally admitted the fact that Obama was indeed an American citizen (something he undoubtedly already knew), he and his staff redirected their energies to keep their conservative right-wing base pacified (Stickings, 2011). Indeed, led by rabid conspiracy theorist Orly Taitz, the birther issue was a highly effective, if not perverse strategy in appealing to America's most jingoistic voting electorate. It was red meat for the nation's most racially afflicted voters. It played right into their sordid and largely unhinged psyches. A highly exploitative issue for sure (Mundy, 2009).

The reality is that there is a sizable segment of the White American population (as well as some non-White Americans) that could not come to grips with the fact that the nation actually elected a Black man as president, and still cannot even after he has left office. To these men and women, a Black president is a fantasy, an image solely relegated to literature, Hollywood movies, and other fictional spheres. Not as a real-life figure. To these men and women, having a Black man as leader of the free world was/is incomprehensible. For the bigoted, it is an affront to both their racial sensibilities and to the sort of Jim Crow America they love to envision. One that was largely free of deeply entrenched multiculturalism and a semblance of equality (Nazaryan, 2017).

Polling, at the time, demonstrated that many politically right-of-center Americans, particularly conservative voters, were skeptical of

President Obama's American citizenship. Interestingly, an NBC News/ Survey Monkey Poll conducted that summer found that 80 percent of Democrats agreed with the statement that "Barack Obama was born in the United States," while 41 percent of Republicans disagreed with it (Clinton & Roush, 2016).

The truth is that many liberal and progressive voters were not totally enamored with President Obama. A number of his left of center critics had substantial disagreements with him that were based on policy and a few of his more conservative detractors had significant policy disagreements with him that were based on ideology and not necessarily based on racial animus. Nonetheless, the fact is the birther movement was/is grounded in racial animosity and many supporters and members of the birther movement were motivated by racism. Trump's sudden disavowal and closing the chapter of his long-held "belief" did little, if anything, to assuage the more die hard and adamantly bigoted detractors of the president that Barack Obama was indeed born on American soil.

REFERENCES

Clinton, Josh, & Roush, Carrie (2016, August 10). Poll: Persistent partisan divide over "birther" question. *NBC News*. Retrieved from https://www.nbcnews.com/politics/2016-election/poll-persistent-partisan-divide-over-birther-question-n627446

Edroso, Roy (2016, September 19). Right bloggers finally go off birtherism — Once Trump blames it on Hillary. *Village Voice*.

Glass, Nick (2016, September 15). Trump concedes Obama was born in the U.S. *Politico*. Retrieved from https://www.politico.com/story/2016/09/donald-trump-birtherism-campaign-statement-228261

Mundy, Liza (2009, October 6). Orly Taitz's crusade to challenge President Obama's legitimacy. *Washington Post*. Retrieved from http://www.washingtonpost.com/wp-dyn/content/article/2009/10/05/AR2009100503819.html.

Nazaryan, Alexander (2017, August 28). Donald Trump and Joe Arpaio: A bromance forged in birtherism and xenophobia. *Newsweek Magazine*. Retrieved from https://www.newsweek.com/trump-arpaio-pardon-arizona-maricopa-immigration-655995

Rees, Annie (2016, September 22). Former RNC chair: Trump's birtherism is "bullshit racism". *Talking Points Memo*. Retrieved from https://talkingpointsmemo.com/livewire/former-rnc-chairman-michael-steele-trump-birtherism-bullshit-racism

Smith, Ben, & Tau, Byron (2011, April 22). Birtherism: Where it all began. *Politico.* Retrieved from https://www.politico.com/story/2011/04/birtherism-where-it-all-began-053563

Stickings, Michael J. W. (2011, April 22). Birtherism, bullshit and Donald Trump. *The Reaction Blogspot.* Retrieved from https://the-reaction.blogspot.com/2011/04/birtherism-bullshit-and-donald-trump.html

7

Michelle Obama: Playa Hatin' on the Former First Lady

From the moment her husband became a serious contender for the Democratic nomination, Michelle Obama became a perennial figure in the media spotlight. With this level of exposure also came a significant amount of controversy. Unlike previous first ladies such as Rosalyn Carter, the late former first lady, Claudia "Lady Bird" Johnson, Pat Nixon, and others, Mrs. Obama seems to evoke rabid passion among her supporters and detractors alike. There is no middle ground or indifference in their feelings toward her. Her proponents see her as intelligent, classy, elegant, no-nonsense, charismatic, and socially conscious. Her opponents denounce her as being arrogant, aloof, unpatriotic, and racially bigoted and harboring a socialist agenda (Parton, 2015).

For her critics, the already high level of suspicion toward both Obamas reached a fever pitch in the 2008 presidential campaign when the then-future first lady stated that for the first time in her adult life she was really proud of America. While many reasonable and rational people totally understood what she meant (even Laura Bush later in the same year in an interview stated that she did) and were well aware of the fact that there was not one hint of unpatriotic rhetoric in her comments, the political right wasted no time in perversely exploiting a sincere statement, misconstruing it to imply that Mrs. Obama was an anti-American who harbored Black nationalist sentiments.

Sensing a possible campaign issue, the Republican right seized on Mrs. Obama, making her the target of vicious assaults. She was accused of hating Whites and using the term "whitey" on tape. Terms such as "baby mama," "angry Black woman," "Jezebel," "Black Lady Macbeth," "Modern Day Marie

Antoinette" (Montopoli, 2010), "ape in heels" (Phillips, 2016), "Ms. Griev-ance," "bitch" (in many cases preceded by the word Black), "uppity," and other derogatory and disrespectful labels were ascribed to her (Kelly, 2009). In fact, on some far right–wing websites, the language used to describe both her and her husband was so inflammatory and intolerant that some website moderators decided to shut down for a few days to reissue stricter guidelines for bloggers. I could/would not even repeat such incendiary rhetoric here.

Not content enough to just take a quote grossly out of context, the anti-Michelle crowd posted copies of her Princeton undergraduate thesis on anti-Obama websites in an effort to demonstrate that she was obsessed with being Black, attacked her University of Chicago administrative job as a "diversity position," decried her 2015 commencement speech at Tuskeegee University (Hannagan, 2015), spread false rumors that she only wanted Black and other non-Whites at campaign rallies, that she was on tape yell-ing anti-American statements, and other such nonsense (Case, 2015). A couple of talk show hosts referred to Michelle Obama by invoking the term "lynching party." Yes indeed, things were getting ugly. The McCain campaign fall rallies demonstrated the vile, seething anti-Obama paranoia and hatred that was evident.

With regard to the supposed tapes, the interesting thing is that none of them ever surfaced. This is probably due to the fact that no such tapes likely ever existed. The Republican architects of such sinister schemes were well aware of this; however, they knew that it was not necessary for them to produce any concrete evidence. For their jingoistic, wild-eyed, racist, sexist, xenophobic right-winged supporters, just the thought of such images was enough to whip them into an anti-Michelle Obama frenzy.

Some people argue that there have been other former first ladies like Hillary Clinton and Nancy Reagan who have undergone critical and hostile scrutiny. While true, neither Mrs. Clinton nor Mrs. Reagan were subjected to acerbic racial overtones. They were criticized for certain excesses, but never were the attacks, especially in the case of Nancy Reagan, so racially charged or personal. Race has undoubtedly been a factor in such treatment.

In several post-first lady interviews, she conceded that such malicious attacks did indeed sting at times. However, like many strong, radiant, and viable Black women before her, Mrs. Obama managed to admirably forge on in spite of such vile criticism and resentment and focused on the goals that were/are important to her, such as speaking to young girls in elementary and middle schools and meeting with military families.

Throughout her tenure as first lady, Ms. Obama charmed the world with her impeccable fashion sense. She warmly embraced Queen Elizabeth (the queen reciprocated). She demonstrated that she was just as elegant as any European leader's wife and endeared herself into the minds and hearts of millions of people all over the world. In fact, many people compared her to a previous first lady, Jackie Kennedy.

It appears that this deep admiration for her will remain for quite some time. Now as a former first lady, her popularity is as strong as ever. It seems that many individuals see her diverse, flexible, sincere personality as one that is refreshing to them. Recently, even her most strident, bigoted critics, a number of whom would rather have had her cleaning their homes as opposed to living in the White House, were unable to effectively demonize her. One thing that is probably for certain is that Michelle Obama, now in her post–White house era, will remain true to herself and to her constituencies. She is indeed one classy, resilient, intelligent lady who represented the nation in admirable fashion.

REFERENCES

Anon. (2017, July 27). Michelle Obama discussed emotional scars from critics. *Associated Press*. Retrieved from https://www.voanews.com/a/michelle-obama-emotional-scars/3961277.html

Case, Ellis (2015, May 23). Critics of first lady Michelle Obama double down. *USA Today*. Retrieved from https://eu.news-leader.com/story/opinion/contributors/2015/05/23/critics-first-lady-michelle-obama-double/27853389/

Hannagan, Charley (2015, May 13). Critics lash out at Michelle Obama's Tuskegee University speech (What they're saying). *Syracuse*. Retrieved from https://www.syracuse.com/opinion/index.ssf/2015/05/critics_lash_out_at_michelle_obamas_tuskegee_university_speech_what_theyre_sayin.html

Kelly, Chris (2009, April 23). Townhall: Michelle Obama is a bitch, get it? *Huffington Post*. Retrieved from https://www.huffingtonpost.com/chris-kelly/townhall-michelle-obama-i_b_177947.html

Montopoli, Brian (2010, August 5). Michelle Obama criticized as modern day Marie Antoinette over Spain vacation. Retrieved from https://www.cbsnews.com/news/michelle-obama-criticized-as-modern-day-marie-antoinette-over-spain-vacation/

Parton, Heather Digby (2015, September 9). The right wing's hideous crusade against Michelle Obama has completely fallen apart. *Salon*. Retrieved from https://www.salon.com/2015/09/03/the_right_wings_hideous_crusade_against_michelle_obama_has_completely_fallen_apart/

Phillips, Kristine (2016, December 27). The non-profit director who called Michelle Obama an ape in heels has lost her job — For good. *The Washington Post*. Retrieved from https://www.washingtonpost.com/news/post-nation/wp/2016/12/27/the-nonprofit-director-who-called-michelle-obama-an-ape-in-heels-has-lost-her-job-for-good/?utm_term=.16e1c1fe6623

8

Denial of Supreme Court Seat: One of a Long Line of Racial Slights toward President Obama

By 2016, the last full year of his presidency, just when you thought that the level of mean-spirited arrogance directed toward President Obama could not get any more disgraceful, a new example came along to add to a long list of slights and disrespectful behavior. The late Supreme Court Associate Justice Antonin Scalia's body was barely cold before a civil war of words began to make the rounds throughout Washington and the nation at large.

Anyone who follows politics likely has indelible memories of the verbal grenades that a number of Republican politicians hurled (some still do in his post-presidency) toward President Obama during the winter of 2016. Senate majority leader Mitch McConnell arrogantly stated in no uncertain terms that the Senate would not entertain the idea of voting for any Supreme Court nominee that President Obama would submit for confirmation (Raju, Barrett, & LoBianco, 2016).

Imagine that, telling the leader of the free world to basically "forget it," we are not going to consider, let alone confirm any Supreme Court nominee you put forth. There were conservative operatives such as 2016 GOP presidential candidates Marco Rubio and Ted Cruz and others who attempted to make arguments (unconvincingly) by either inadvertently or purposely misinterpreting the Constitution in an effort to give credence to the position they had staked out in an effort to curry favor with their right-wing constituencies. It was a sad, bemusing commentary for sure.

Needless to say, when the smoke cleared, there was a more fundamental reason for the level of blatant disrespect and obstruction that confronted

President Obama during his tenure as the nation's first Black president — race. It's that simple. From the minute he was sworn in as the nation's 44th president, this president (and, in some cases, his wife) were the victim(s) of unrelenting vitriol from a segment of the population that immediately became emotionally unhinged at the reality of a Black man and his family residing at 1600 Pennsylvania Avenue.

There are those who will argue that all presidents, particularly recent presidents, have been subjected to varied forms of disrespectful behavior from political opposition to the public at large. While there is some kernel of truth to this, the fact is that, in the case of Obama, such disrespectful behavior was taken to an entirely new level. The insults were more searing, deep-seated, and acidic.

In some quarters, the former president has been held in such ill regard that some journalists, political pundits, cultural critics, and even fellow politicians routinely made it their duty to remind the public of such treatment. Well, right here, right now, I am doing the same! To refresh your memory here are examples of how our former commander-in-chief was treated with such contempt:

The fraudulent birther issue led by Orly Taitz and championed by then presidential candidate Donald Trump — now President Trump — that raised questions about the president's citizenship.

Mitch McConnell, at the time Senate minority leader, boldly announcing that the priority for the Republican Party was to make Barack Obama a one-term president.

Congressman Joe Wilson (R-S.C.) yelling "you lie" at President Obama during his State of the Union speech in 2010.

Tea Party signs that displayed blatant and venomous racism in their anti-Obama statements.

The House GOP prompted by the Tea Party refusing to raise the debt ceiling in 2011.

The House GOP — before notifying the White House — invited Israeli Prime Minister Benjamin Netanyahu to address a joint session to denounce negotiations with Iran on limiting its nuclear program.

Former Arizona governor Jan Brewer directly shaking her finger in the president's face.

Newt Gingrich referring to the president's "anti-colonial behavior."

President Trump accusing Obama of spying on him during the election and creating a mess for him (Trump) to inherit.

The list goes on and on.

To add insult to injury, Trump is doing everything in his power (with an all too eager Republican congress) to dismantle President Obama's legacy (Walsh, 2017).

While naysayers can belabor the point of other presidents being targets of hostility, the fact is that no other president in recent memory has been subjected to such dishonorable behavior. It is clear that race has been the predominant factor.

In February 2016 on MSNBC's Hardball with Chris Matthews, Matthews had as his guest Harvard law professor Lawrence Tribe. Both men said that there were a number of Republicans and segments of the White population who were determined to mark the Obama presidency with an asterisk, that they wanted future generations of Americans to view this president as somehow "illegitimate" (Hardball, 2016).

There was certainly considerable evidence for such an argument. Even former Supreme Court Justice Sandra Day O'Connor, a Reagan nominee, expressed her dismay with the actions of some Senate Republicans, condemned such behavior, and made a passionate, strong case for the process of choosing and confirming a justice to proceed quickly. Months and in some cases, more than a year later, once the Merrick Garland nomination was officially dead (Ware, 2017), several newspapers (*New York Times*, 2016) and a number of political pundits gathered together to discuss such unprecedented and shameful behavior by congress (Millhisher, Aron, & Goodman, 2017).

The fact is that many Whites, particularly those over 60, came of age in an America where people like them, particularly White men, were the people who made decisions. Other people, especially non-Whites, were seen but not heard and were, oftentimes, invisible to the mind. Shifting demographic trends over the past few decades have caused deep psychological anxiety among more than a few individuals. The days of pre-1980 yesteryear are becoming a distant and fading memory.

That being said, it was certainly frustrating to see President Obama (too often as far as I am concerned) hold back from calling out such behavior for what it was. Rather than confront such racism, he often reverted to engaging in a form of an "it's partly my fault" position. It was as if he had become afflicted with a mild degree of Stockholm Syndrome. This was disappointing. Though, as many pointed out, he was aware that he was walking a very fine line being the nation's first Black president.

The fact is that no one is perfect. We can spin, analyze, deflect, deny, decry, etc., but history and the truth will reveal that the majority of resistance, and less than cordial treatment, that President Obama confronted on this specific issue (along with many others) was due to his race, period. Something tells me that he was probably smart enough to know this.

REFERENCES

Editorial Board (2016, December 24). The stolen Supreme Court seat. *New York Times*. Retrieved from https://www.nytimes.com/2016/12/24/opinion/sunday/the-stolen-supreme-court-seat.html

Matthews, Chris (2016, February 15). Hardball with Chris Matthews, transcript: Guests — Dana Milbank, Abby Phillip, Paul Singer, Hillary Clinton, Richard Blumenthal, Laurenee Tribe. Retrieved from http://www.msnbc.com/transcripts/hardball/2016-02-15

Millhisher, John, Aron, Nan, & Goodman, Amy (2017, February 1). "Stolen Seat": A look on how Republicans blocked Obama's Supreme Court nominee. *Democracy Now!*. Retrieved from https://www.democracynow.org/2017/2/1/stolen_seat_a_look_back_on

Raju, Manu, Barrett, Ted, & LoBianco, Tom (2016, February 23). Senate GOP: No hearings for Supreme Court nominee. *CNN*. Retrieved from https://edition.cnn.com/2016/02/23/politics/joe-biden-supreme-court-senate-republicans/index.html

Walsh, Kenneth T. (2017, June 30). The never-ending ending duel. *U.S. News and World Report*. Retrieved from https://www.usnews.com/news/the-report/articles/2017-06-30/trumps-attacks-on-obama-show-how-hostile-the-nation-is

Ware, Doug (2017, January 3). Nomination expires for Obama Supreme Court appointee Merrick Garland. Retrieved from https://www.upi.com/Top_News/US/2017/01/03/Nomination-expires-for-Obama-Supreme-Court-appointee-Merrick-Garland/4841483472115/

9

The Intersection of Racial, Gender, and Economic Politics

For some people, November 8, 2016 was one of the greatest days in American history. Others may very well see it as a day that will live in political infamy. The 2016 presidential election was over, and Donald John Trump had been elected as the 45th president of the United States of America.

If people are being honest with themselves, most people, save for a few like Michael Moore who had predicted the real possibility of Trump winning the presidential election more than a year ago, did not see this coming (Moore, 2016). The American political establishment, large swaths of the American public, and the entire world were shocked and stunned by Trump's triumph (Goldmacher & Scheckinger, 2016). While Hillary Clinton did win the popular vote, Trump carried the electoral college that ultimately determines who wins the presidency.

When it became clear that battleground and bellwether states were consistently dropping into the GOP column, what was once seen as intense enthusiasm rapidly dissipated in many liberal circles and unhinged delirium engulfed in conservative quarters. When the initial shock settled, many individuals, both inside and outside the media, engaged in fierce Wednesday, Thursday, Friday morning, afternoon, and evening quarterbacking. Various scenarios and theories were bandied about as to how such an outcome could have possibly occurred. While the truth is that there are likely many reasons as to why so many people, specifically White people, voted for Donald Trump, I would argue that some of the more rational ones are:

- *Economic populism*: Through various periods in our nation's history, charismatic politicians espousing a populist message have sporadically emerged onto the political scene garnering the support of those citizens who feel disenfranchised or left behind. Both Trump and Bernie Sanders tapped into the intense populist tsunami that was raging throughout the nation. Both men fervently discussed economic marginalization, were critical of outsourcing jobs, Wall Street, unchecked globalization, neo-liberalism, and other factors they saw as contributing to the demise of many working-class people. The major difference was that Trump tinged his message with a dangerously high level of jingoism and nationalism.

- *Racial, cultural, and gender resentment*: Proving W. E. B. Du Bois' prediction from *The Souls of Black Folk* (DuBois, 1903) – that race would be the definitive issue of the twentieth century – are twenty-first-century American politics. In particular, to be blunt and to keep it real, the Trump campaign engaged in a blatantly racist, sexist, shameless, divisive campaign. They preyed upon and exploited the fears of Whites who were fearful and resentful of immigration, affirmative action (despite the fact that White people, especially White women, are the biggest beneficiaries of the policy), multiculturalism, gay marriage, and other issues that are often seen as anathema to a number of racist, sexist, homophobic, anti-Semitic, xenophobic members in this group. The fact that the alt-right and well-known White nationalists like David Duke and Steven Bannon of Breitbart.com either praised or were active members of his campaign was alarming in and of itself. Many male members of this group were likely resentful of the prospect of a woman becoming commander-in-chief. By no means did all people who supported Trump harbor such viewpoints — likely many did not — but a sizable number did. It is notable to point out that the majority of Whites across age groups from senior citizens to millennials voted for Trump. CNN commentator Van Jones said it best that Trump's victory was due in part to a "whitelash" (Ryan, 2016).

- *The news media*: Years later, while there seems to be some remorse in certain quarters of the press, the fact is that the mainstream media largely contributed to Donald Trump's success. His antics, theatrics, and often unpredictable behavior became a lucrative engine for many segments of the media, in that it afforded them the opportunity to generate megabucks in advertising revenue. They would often let him go off on tangents about various topics without challenging him to verify his statements as they required of other candidates. It is also probably safe to say that the press was largely unprepared to cover a presidential candidate who was already a professional media celebrity. He was able to successfully manipulate much of the press core. There were other factors.

Despite winning the popular vote, Hillary Clinton's negatives (as were Trump's) were still considerably high for a candidate running for public office. Moreover, her political enemies were able to paint her as a person who was seen as secretive, polarizing, untrustworthy, lacking in integrity, etc. The FBI "October Surprise" that turned out to be a false alarm by director James Comey certainly did not help soothe largely negative perceptions and suspicions deeply ingrained in the minds of many of her detractors and even a few allies (Allen & Parnes, 2016). She simply carried too much baggage from her past history (Cooper, 2017).

Despite all the drama, the undeniable truth is that the 2016 presidential campaign was, indeed, one of the most surprising, exciting, unpredictable, and, at times, jarring elections in American political history. It will certainly be one that will be discussed for a very long time to come.

REFERENCES

Allen, Jonathan, & Parnes, Amie (2016). *Shattered: Inside Hillary Clinton's doomed campaign.* New York, NY: Crown Books. Introduction.

Cooper, Matthew (2017, May 9). Why Hillary Clinton lost to Donald Trump. Retrieved from newsweekmagazine.com.

DuBois, W. E. B. (1903). *The souls of black folk: Essays and sketches.* Chicago, IL: A.G. McClure Publishers.

Goldmacher, Shane, & Scheckinger, Ben (2016, November 9). Trump pulls off biggest upset in U.S. history. *Politico.* Retrieved from https://www.politico.com/story/2016/11/election-results-2016-clinton-trump-231070.

Moore, Michael (2016, July 23). 5 Reasons why Trump will win. *Huffington Post.* Retrieved from https://www.huffingtonpost.com/michael-moore/5-reasons-why-trump-will-_b_11156794.html

Ryan, Josiah (2016, November 9). This was a whitelash: Van Jones take on the election results. *CNN.* Retrieved from https://edition.cnn.com/2016/11/09/politics/van-jones-results-disappointment-cnntv/index.html

10

The Alt-Right and the Repulsive Spirit of White Supremacy

In August 2017, millions of Americans (and international viewers) were witness to the horrendous drama and carnage that occurred in Charlottesville, Virginia. We witnessed hundreds of young White men (and some women, though overwhelmingly male) march through the streets of this university town with torches, chanting "blood and soil," "Jews will not replace us," "You will not replace us" (referring to non-Whites). Such ominous rhetoric was eerily reminiscent of the Nuremberg marches commonplace in Nazi Germany in the 1930s. It was a dramatic spectacle to behold.

The violence that occurred on that Saturday morning and continued into the afternoon, August 12, was even more harrowing (Heim, 2017). Viewers saw Klan sympathizers and neo-Nazis battle it out with anti-racist activists in the streets. Racial epithets were espoused. Clergy members were attacked. Individual people were pepper sprayed. People were trampled and thrown to the ground. Mayhem was the order of the day. Such wanton violence culminated with the death of Heather Heyer, a 32-year-old paralegal and native of Charlottesville (Caron, 2017). Several others were critically injured.

James Field, a 20-year-old Ohio native and a young man with strong ties to White supremacist groups was the perpetrator of such sadistic violence (Stolberg & Rosenthal, 2017). Two other state troopers died when the helicopter they were flying in crashed in the woods. Fields was charged with first-degree murder along with several other charges (Anon., 2017). President Trump weighed in on the event with tepid comments directing criticism at "both sides" for their hatred, and made the case that there were "very fine people" who participated in such a horrendous spectacle (Reilly, 2017).

Understandably, such intellectually dishonest comments disturbed and angered many people on both sides of the political aisle, but earned the praise of White supremacists (Nussbaum, 2017) and caused a firestorm of outrage (Stange, 2017). Indeed, for a President in the twenty-first century (or any era), to give praise and provide cover for White supremacists was one of the most odious acts that one can imagine. It is unconscionable.

The undisputed truth is that there is absolutely no moral equation or comparison between rabid White supremacists who rallied in Charlottesville spewing racial and religious hatred and the protesters who, for the most part, demonstrated peacefully but were attacked for some reason by a mentally disturbed, racist madman (Hauslohner, Duggen, Gillum, & Davis, 2017). These several hundred White supremacists descended upon a prestigious college town espousing hatred against Blacks, Jews, non-Whites, perversely talking about blood and soil and the right to arm themselves to the teeth regardless of consequences. They arrogantly and shamelessly praised Adolf Hitler and unflinchingly gave Nazi salutes. They had/have no apprehension in reveling in the sordid history of the Confederacy and avidly support similarly retrograde causes. Some have gone as far as to participate in domestic terrorism.

The right-wing protests in Charlottesville did not happen overnight. They are the culmination of ongoing and careless rhetoric that has festered in certain isolated quarters in our culture and has more recently been allowed to manifest itself in the larger society. Indeed, over the past few years, the nation has witnessed many such incidents: James Jackson, a then 28-year-old White racist obsessed with a hatred of Black men attacked and murdered a 66-year-old Black man, Timothy Caughman, with a sword in New York City (Domonoske, 2017). The senseless killing of 23-year-old Lieutenant Richard Collins, an extremely young, accomplished Black man in Maryland, by Sean Urbanski, a member of the alt-Reich Nation (Zirin, 2017). A deranged human, Adam Puninton, opening fire on two immigrants, Srinivas Kuchibhotla and Ashish Vaidya in Kansas, killing Kuchibhotla. The double homicide and wounding of Richard John Best. Two White men, Ricky John Best and Taliesin Myrddin Nankai Meche were savagely murdered in Portland, Oregon, and another, Micah Fletcher, was severely wounded by White supremacist Jeremy Joseph Christensen, when they came to the defense of a young Muslim woman and her Black friend (Dobuzinsky, 2017). Nooses found at the National Museum of African History and Culture (Williams & McGlone, 2017). The list goes on. The Internet has afforded the alt-right the opportunity to mobilize in a manner that would have been unimaginable a few decades ago, and its members have indeed capitalized on this opportunity (Collins, 2017).

Donald Trump and his circle have contributed to and engineered a climate of hostility. Initially staffing his administration with the right-wing ideologues like Steven Bannon, Stephen Miller (the two sinister Steves), Sebastian Gorka (both Bannon and Gorka eventually left), and Jeff Sessions (although the attorney general's statements on the Charlottesville incident and White supremacists was a welcome, if not latent response, his other decisions have been deplorable) and other like-minded folks further emboldened the alt-right and other far right–wing organizations.

Trump rallied onto the political scene in early 2016 with many aggressive, harsh, and politically retrograde messages. Racism, sexism, and xenophobia were common staples throughout his odiously divisive candidacy. While there are multiple examples of irresponsible rhetoric that have emanated from Trump's campaign, the most striking and pointed message has been his promise to "Make America Great Again." While such a statement can mean varied things and have multiple meanings to many people, the message that Trump was espousing to his largely right-of-center, Tea Party, birther-obsessed crowd, and, to many of us who are non-White, was an unambiguous, unapologetic return to a time when White people, in particular, White men, were in control. Such an unflinching narrative was brilliantly explained in a phenomenally well-written, meticulously researched, and admirably detailed article by journalist Adam Serwer (Serwer, 2017).

Indeed, Trump has fed very tasty T-bone steaks to more than a few White men (and some women for that matter, for after all, he received 53 percent of the White female vote in 2016 among White women who voted). Many of these women harbor White nationalist sympathies (Darby, 2017), who long for the days when heterosexual, able-bodied White men ruled and where Latino and other dark-skinned, non-White immigrants were largely non-existent. A world where Blacks and, in some cases, Jews, were occasionally seen, certainly not heard from, and deprived of any sense of dignity, fairness, and equality. Women were largely relegated to second-class status, were of no competition in the workplace, had to often quietly overlook or turn a blind eye to infidelity or spousal abuse, and were largely relegated to objects of sexual objectification. Gays and lesbians were seen as less than human, regarded as deviants, perverts, and unworthy of any form of respect. Disabled people were seen as quasi-human, burdensome, and semi-tragic figures. Yes, for a sizable percentage of this segment of American society, these were indeed the "good ol' days" (Khazan, 2017).

While such a reality really never existed for many Whites (in particular, lower income and poor Whites and certainly not White women across socio-economic backgrounds), the fact is that more than a few Whites have been deluded into believing that such an America of yesteryear did exist to their benefit. This is particularly true of the economically disaffected segment of White America who avidly supported Donald Trump for President. In 2016, Trump and his minions were able to effectively capitalize on the misguided fears and resentment of this voting block to effectively win their way to the White house (Neiwert, 2017). They have abused and misused their power ever since.

The fact is that we are indeed living in perilous times. The nation has passed a crossroads. America is becoming ever more polarized to a degree that is poised to make the first decade of the twenty-first century look like a United Colors of Benetton advertisement. Sadly, President Trump shows no signs of rejecting the rhetoric of those around him who are likely whispering seeds of division and discord in his ear, and rather, refraining from engaging in "us vs them" behavior. Now, more than two years into his presidency, there is no reason to believe that he will come to the realization that he could be much more effective by embracing those who seek an America that is one of unification and inclusion. Quite frankly, his far right wing political base would likely become incensed if he were to adhere to such a sagacious message.

As the nation increasingly fragments, America can ill afford to continue down such a dark tunnel of fear, hostility, resentment, hatred, and uncertainty. These are the only things that the alt-right (White supremacists) and others of their retrograde ilk have to offer.

REFERENCES

Anon. (2017, August 18). Fields faces 5 additional felony charges related to August 12 fatal crash. Retrieved from dailyprogress.com.

Caron, Christina (2017, August 13). Heather Heyer, Charlottesville victim, is recalled as "a strong woman". *New York Times*. Retrieved from https://www.nytimes.com/2017/08/13/us/heather-heyer-charlottesville-victim.html

Collins, Cory (2017, Fall). What is the "Alt-Right"? *Teaching Tolerance*, 57. Retrieved from https://www.tolerance.org/magazine/fall-2017/what-is-the-altright

Darby, Seyward (2017, September). The rise of the Valkyries in the Alt Right women are the future and the problem. *Harper's Magazine*. Retrieved from https://harpers.org/archive/2017/09/the-rise-of-the-valkyries/

Dobuzinsky, Alex (2017, May 27). Two men stabbed to death on Oregon train trying to stop anti-Muslim rant. *Reuters.com*. Retrieved from https://www.reuters.com/article/us-usa-muslims-portland/two-men-stabbed-to-death-on-oregon-train-trying-to-stop-anti-muslim-rant-idUSKBN18N080

Domonoske, Camile (2017, March 28). White supremacist charged with terrorism over murder of black man. *NPR News*. Retrieved from https://www.npr.org/sections/thetwo-way/2017/03/28/521805165/white-supremacist-charged-with-terrorism-over-murder-of-black-man

Hauslohner, Abigail, Duggen, Paul, Gillum, Jack, & Davis, Aaron C. (2017, August 18). James Fields Jr. a neo-Nazi's violent rage-fueled journey to Charlottesville. *The Washington Post*. Retrieved from https://www.washingtonpost.com/local/trafficandcommuting/a-neo-nazis-rage-fueled-journey-to-charlottesville/2017/08/18/a7e881fa-8296-11e7-902a-2a9f2d808496_story.html?noredirect=on&utm_term=.8fffa26be59d

Heim, Joe (2017, August 14). Recounting a day of rage, hate, violence and death. *The Washington Post*. Retrieved from https://www.washingtonpost.com/graphics/2017/local/charlottesville-timeline/?utm_term=.ced5524c30ba

Khazan, Olga (2017, August 17). The dark minds of the Alt-Right. *The Atlantic*. Retrieved from https://www.theatlantic.com/science/archive/2017/08/the-dark-minds-of-the-alt-right/537144/

Neiwert, David (2017). *Alt-America: The rise of the radical right in the age of Trump*. New York, NY: Verso Press.

Nussbaum, Matthew (2017, August 15). Trump goes off script, and White supremacists cheer. *Politico*. Retrieved from https://www.politico.com/story/2017/08/15/trump-white-supremacists-charlottesville-241672

Reilly, Katie (2017, August 15). White supremacists loved President Trump's latest comments on Charlottesville. *TIME* Retrieved from timemagazine.com.

Serwer, Adam (2017, November 20). The nationalist's delusion. *The Atlantic*. Retrieved from https://www.theatlantic.com/politics/archive/2017/11/the-nationalists-delusion/546356/

Stange, Niall (2017, August 16). The memo: Trump reignites race firestorm. *The Hill*. Retrieved from https://thehill.com/homenews/administration/346712-the-memo-trump-reignites-race-firestorm

Stevens, Matt (2017, June 9). Kansas man indicted on hate crime charges in shooting of Indian immigrants. *New York Times*. Retrieved from https://

www.nytimes.com/2017/06/09/us/indian-immigrants-kansas-hate-crime.html

Stolberg, Sheryl Gay, & Rosenthal, Brian M. (2017, August 12). Man charged after White Nationalist Rally in Charlottesville ends in deadly violence. *New York Times*. Retrieved from https://www.nytimes.com/2017/08/12/us/charlottesville-protest-white-nationalist.html.

Williams, Clarence, & McGlone, Peggy (2017, June 1). Noose found at exhibit in African American Smithsonian Museum. *The Washington Post*. Retrieved from https://www.washingtonpost.com/local/public-safety/noose-found-at-exhibit-in-african-american-smithsonian-museum/2017/05/31/ce0eccf6-464e-11e7-a196-a1bb629f64cb_story.html?utm_term=.43919867a244

Zirin, Dave (2017, May 22). A lynching on the University of Maryland campus. *The Nation*. Retrieved from https://www.thenation.com/article/lynching-university-maryland-campus/

PART II

Staying Woke!

11

Authentically Black: The Debate Lives On

At various stages during his tenure as president, Barack Obama waded into the often precarious "acting White" debate. This fact was directly confronted in 2014 when he responded to a question from a young Native American man who inquired as to what the federal government was doing to help his ethnic group "revitalize their language and culture." The former president, in his usual measured and thoughtful comments, responded in somewhat pastoral terms as he quoted the bible, commenting that "without a vision, people will perish," and how an absence of such an identity can lead to further erosion of one's physical, psychological, and emotional health. That being said he later transitioned into a DuBoisian (W. E. B. DuBois) moment when he told the young person in question that there was nothing irregular or counterfeit for a person to further embrace the larger culture while simultaneously celebrating and preserving their own. In short, there was/is nothing wrong with being bi-cultural or embracing the practice of acculturation.

A number of media outlets from the conservative editorial page of the *Wall Street Journal* to op-ed columnists from the *Washington Post* (Valbrun, 2007), *New York Times*, other national newspapers, and a few academics (Japtok & Jenkins, 2011) weighed in on what they saw as President Obama reigniting the "acting White" controversy (Watson, 2014). For the record, the anti-Obama *Wall Street Journal* broke from their regular adversarial stance and praised the president and his administration for establishing the program. There were others like blogger, former CNN commentator and frequent Obama critic and acerbic radio host Dr. Boyce Watkins, who argued that the program appeared to be too broad without any specific focus" (Muhammad & Muhammad, 2014). Watkins further argued that Obama, his administration, and inner circle failed to address the issue of persistent discrimination and chronic unemployment that plagued large portions of the Black community, particularly lower-income and urban communities.

That being said, it was interesting and very telling that the majority of political and cultural pundits who commented on the subject focused on what they saw as the "acting White" assumption being brought back to the forefront of political and social debate. It is a subject that sporadically reemerges at the forefront of debates in many segments of the Black community. In 2011, the topic was rife in the Black blogosphere (and social media in general) after NBA basketball star Grant Hill masterfully and eloquently responded to Jalen Rose's critical comments directed toward him (Grant) and other Black athletes (and Black people in general) who were/are the products of more upscale and privileged backgrounds (Hill, 2011).

Speaking of sports, I still have not forgotten the unhinged tirade of former ESPN commentator Robert Parker several years ago as he launched into a vicious, condescending tirade attacking NFL player Robert Griffith demanding to know whether Griffith was a "real brother" or a "cornball brother." Parker was more specifically attacking what was rumored to be Griffith's Republican Party political affiliation, his then White fiancé, and what he perceived to be his (Griffith's) other supposed "misguided" decisions (Williams, 2012). After hearing such a screed, you would have thought that Parker was one of the gatekeepers of Blackness and a card carrying member of the Black thought police. Reaction to Parker (from people of all races) was swift and he was dismissed from ESPN soon afterward (Grant, 2013).

Speaking closer to home, I wonder if someone like myself who likes to listen to Peter Frampton, Bryan Adams, Band of Horses, One Republic, and Irish music is in the "danger zone" of losing one's authentic Blackness. Perhaps, it might be best for me to shout from the mountaintops that I also love gospel music. Cry passionate alligator tears that I love a fair amount of jazz and blues music. Swear on a stack of bibles that I actually do love the late Michael Jackson (as do many White people), adore James Brown, Aretha Franklin, as well as classic R&B and soul music in general. Truth be told, the fact is that Irish music is, indeed, very soulful. It is the European version of Black gospel music.

Not to add insult to injury, but I am a voracious reader, and, sometimes, I read books that are absent of Black subject matter! For the diehard members of the Black thought militia, I have probably come close to committing racial treason. I am a "suspect" negro so to speak, or at the very least, unreliable and largely artificial. After all, in their eyes, deviating from such supposedly "authentic Black" behavior may have almost certainly qualified me as a prime candidate for a Dave Chapelle skit.

Goodness knows if it were any group of people who should know how demeaning it is to be pre-judged, be passed judgment on, assumed on how you will behave, how you think, how intelligent you are (or supposedly not), etc., based on the pigmentation of your skin, it is Black people. Yet, some (not all, by any means, but probably too many of us) from barbershops to beauty shops, to houses of worship to soul food diners and other similar venues, have no hesitation in engaging in racial histrionics, sitting around passing judgment either ratifying or disqualifying one another based on what are far too often superficial values. The degree of hypocrisy is real!

The hard fact is that all of us who are Black, regardless of socio-economic status or educational level, at some point in our lives will be confronted with the reality that your skin color (minus those few who can choose to pass if they want to) will render you "other" in the eyes of some Whites and some other non-Blacks (Staples, 2017). There is no need to engage in unscientific racial litmus tests to do so. There are enough issues plaguing the Black community, internal as well as external, as it is. We are all pretty much in the same boat. There is no need to add unnecessary baggage.

REFERENCES

Grant, Ethan (2013, January 8). Rob Parker fired: ESPN makes right call in wake of analyst's RG3 commentary. *Bleacher Report*. Retrieved from https://bleacherreport.com/articles/1476298-rob-parker-fired-espn-makes-right-call-in-wake-of-analysts-rg3-commentary

Hill, Grant (2011, March 16). Grant Hill responds to Jalen Rose. *New York Times*. Retrieved from https://thequad.blogs.nytimes.com/2011/03/16/grant-hills-response-to-jalen-rose/

Japtok, Martin, & Jenkins, Jemy R. (2011). *Authentic blackness "Real Blackness": Essays on the meaning of blackness in literature and culture*. New York, NY: Peter Lang Publishers.

Muhammad, Richard B., & Muhammad, Eric T. (2014, March 5). My brother's keeper? Presidential initiative inspires hope, questions. *The Final Call*. Retrieved from http://www.finalcall.com/artman/publish/National_News_2/article_101254.shtml

Staples, Brent (2017, February 11). Editorial observer: Decoding the debate over the blackness of Barack Obama. *New York Times*. Retrieved from https://www.nytimes.com/2007/02/11/opinion/11iht-edstaples.4549121.html

Valbrun, Marjorie (2007, February 16). Black like me? *The Washington Post*. Retrieved from http://www.washingtonpost.com/wp-dyn/content/article/2007/02/15/AR2007021501270.html

Watson, Elwood (2014, August 12). The authentic blackness: Debate still rears its opinionated head. *The Huffington Post*. Retrieved from https://www.huffpost.com/entry/the-authentic-blackness-d_b_5660986

Williams, Juan (2012, December 20). Robert Griffin III, Rob Parker and the sad truth about our racial politics. *Fox News*. Retrieved from https://www.foxnews.com/opinion/robert-griffin-iii-rob-parker-and-the-sad-truth-about-our-racial-politics.

12

Mental Illness: Yes—It Is a Black Thing!

Several years ago, more than two dozen students, mostly Black, were involved in a violent early morning weekend brawl at a local college hangout near the campus where I teach. In our increasingly digital age and our 24/7 media cycle, the news spread like wildfire throughout town in a matter of hours. Moreover, pictures of the melee were supposedly posted on YouTube (I am sure they were, I had no interest in viewing them) for anyone to witness. Several students were arrested and charged with disorderly conduct and other related charges. The fact that students were arrested for such violent behavior was not surprising and quite frankly, expected. What was more notable was the fact it came to light that several of the students involved in such a violent confrontation suffered from mental illness.

Upon hearing this information, I had flashbacks to other recent stories of similar incidents like the September 2013 mass murder rampage by navy shipyard employee Aaron Alexis (Hermann & Marimon, 2013). The gripping saga of Connecticut mother, Miriam Carey, who was obsessed with deluded paranoia that President Obama was directly manipulating and controlling her life (Anon., 2013). The horrific suicide of a 64-year-old Black man from New Jersey, later identified as John Constantino, who doused gasoline over his body, lit a match, and killed himself (Neff, 2013). In each of these cases, the individual was Black.

Needless to say, each of these stories made national headlines. Not surprisingly, much of the blogosphere, including many segments of the Black blogosphere, were rife with intense commentary about these three individuals, whose life unfortunately came to a tragic end. What also came out of this tragic misfortune was the beginning of a dialogue on a topic that has been far too ignored in the Black community — mental illness (Hollie, 2017). While there have been some Black health experts and others who have long warned about the mental health crisis that afflicts a number of Black Americans, more often than not, too many people have dismissed such a disease based on the long-held narrative that Black Americans are, historically, a strong race of people able to withstand any sort of adversity (which has largely been true) and therefore are largely immune from mental illness (Ham, 2012). Rather, mental illness is a dilemma that primarily affects only White people and a few other non-White groups. Such a belief is dangerously misguided.

In fact, according to the American Association of Suicide Study, suicide is the third most common cause for young Blacks between 15 and 24 years of age. The study also confirmed the fact that Black men are five times more likely to commit suicide than Black women. The shocking suicides of iconic legendary Soul Train host Don Cornelius (Samuels & Pelisik, 2012) and superstar linebacker Junior Seau (Farmer, 2013) in 2012 were examples of two seemingly successful, high-achieving Black men who, from outside view, seemed to have it all, yet were internally empty and depressed inside. Their deaths (in particular, Cornelius) sent shock waves throughout the Black community.

While there have long been various stigmas associated with mental illness among people of all races and ethnicities, much of the Black community has largely been dismissive. Specific reasons why we tend to be more reluctant in seeking out treatment than other groups vary. For some Black people, admitting and confronting the fact that he or she suffers from mental illness makes them appear vulnerable. Denial is commonplace (House-worth, 2017). The perception that other people may think of them as being "crazy," "unhinged," etc. is common. For others, religious beliefs can also come into play. There are Black people who feel that prayer is the only form of counseling and medication required to take care of whatever trials and tribulations they are currently going through. Moreover, there is the "keep your personal business your personal business" mindset that some Blacks (not all) harbor, that prevents others from seeking the treatment they need (Coleman, 2016).

Truth be told, it is not really all that surprising that certain Black Americans would suffer from mental health issues, given the disproportionate number of Black people who suffer from racism, poverty, prejudice, personal slights, individual and systematic discrimination, and various other forms of micro aggressions. In some cases, even for those who may be aware of their situation, financial limitations and other factors can be a barrier to seeking quality treatment. Over time, such an untreated diagnosis can likely cause mental and physical deterioration of a person's health. The cold, hard truth is that mental illness is a disease that can be a potentially debilitating enemy to all those afflicted with it, regardless of race or gender, and should (in fact must) be diagnosed and dealt with aggressively.

REFERENCES

Anon. (2012, May 3). Junior Seau dies at 43. *ESPN*. Retrieved from http://www. espn.com/nfl/story/_/id/7882750/junior-seau-former-san-diego-charger-found-dead-cops-probe-suicide

Anon. (2013, October 5). Mariam Carey identified Capitol Hill car chase driver, was taken for mental-health evaluation. *CBS News*. Retrieved from https://www.cbsnews.com/news/miriam-carey-identified-capitol-hill-car-chase-driver-was-taken-for-mental-health-evaluation/

Coleman, Monica A. (2016). *Bipolar faith: A black woman's journal with depression and faith*. New York, NY: Fortress Press.

Farmer, Sam. (2013, January 10). Junior Seau had brain disease when he committed suicide. *Los Angeles Times*. Retrieved from https://www.latimes.com/sports/la-xpm-2013-jan-10-la-sp-sn-junior-seau-brain-20130110-story.html

Ham, Nia (2012, October 1). Black folks and mental health: Why do we suffer in silence? *Ebony*. Retrieved from https://www.ebony.com/health/black-folks-and-mental-health-610/

Hermann, Peter, & Marimon, Anne E. (2013, September 25). Navy yard shooter Aaron Alexis driven by delusion. *The Washington Post*. Retrieved from https://www.washingtonpost.com/local/crime/fbi-police-detail-shooting-na-vy-yard-shooting/2013/09/25/ee321abe-2600-11e3-b3e9-d97fb087acd6_story.html?noredirect=on&utm_term=.7f88b717c2f5

Hollie, Derrick (2017, May 15). It is time to address mental health in the black community. *Huffington Post*. Retrieved from https://www.huffpost.com/entry/its-time-to-address-mental-health-in-the-black-community_b_591a0f64e4b-086d2d0d8d1dd

Houseworth, Kristina (2017, April 27). Addressing mental health in the black community: Don't ignore warning signs of distress. *The Charlotte Post*. Retrieved from http://www.thecharlottepost.com/news/2017/04/27/life-and-religion/addressing-mental-health-in-the-black-community/

Neff, Blake (2013, October 8). Police identify man who set himself on fire. *The Hill*. Retrieved from https://thehill.com/blogs/blog-briefing-room/news/327143-man-who-set-himself-on-fire-is-identified

Samuels, Alison, & Pelisik, Christine (2012, February 2). Legendary "Soul Train" creator Don Cornelius battled demons in final years. *The Daily Beast*. Retrieved from https://www.thedailybeast.com/legendary-soul-train-creator-don-cornelius-battled-demons-in-final-years

Thompson Jr., Dennis (2009, July 13). Depression in the African American community. *Everyday Health*. Retrieved from https://www.everydayhealth.com/depression/african-americans-and-depression.aspx

13

Black Lives Matter Too

It has been all but impossible not to notice the Black Lives Matter movement. From coast to coast its members have made their presence known with their unapologetic, in-your-face message and rhetoric. While the organization has been a force for more than several years, mainstream visibility had largely eluded it. That ended when two of its members, Jacqueline Mara and Marissa Johnson, disrupted presidential candidate Bernie Sanders as he attempted to deliver a speech in Seattle in August 2015 (Basu, 2015). Suddenly, virtually all of the mainstream media became obsessed with the movement. Indeed, a number of journalists have written extensively on their personal investment in the movement (Lowery, 2017).

Reaction to these protesters was immediate and much of it critical. Many detractors, particularly those on the left, characterized the encounter as an attack on a person (Sanders) who had been an ardent supporter of civil rights, marched with Dr. Martin Luther King Jr., and has embraced other progressive measures his entire adult life.

These were the same leftist critics who decried such actions as "disrespectful," "juvenile," and "misguided." Some even went as far as threatening to withdraw their support, financial or otherwise from the movement. To be sure, the ire of these protestors was not solely confined to Sanders. Hillary Clinton, 2016 democratic presidential candidate and eventual party nominee, and Jeb Bush, GOP presidential candidate and former Florida Governor and 2016 GOP candidate, were also confronted by Black Lives Matter activists.

What distinguished this moment of protest from previous acts of civil disobedience was the fact that, in each of these protests, you saw Black activists not merely asking, but rather demanding, results from possible future presidents. Gone was the usual pretense of polite and cordial deference that have often symbolized more recent behavior of Black activism. What we witnessed was an unprecedented level of blunt demands for change not seen in Black movements since the late 1960s when the Black Panthers and other Black activist groups demanded and shouted for revolutionary change. Indeed, in just a few months, BLM became successful in having politicians from both parties address the concerns of Black and brown citizens (Lowery, 2016).

While such attention was/is notable, there were/are a number of Black people who were far from content with the tactics of this movement. Well-known journalist and former civil rights activist Barbara Reynolds penned a much discussed column expressing her dissatisfaction and dismay with the movement in its current state (Reynolds, 2015).

In her *Washington Post* op-ed piece, Reynolds made the case that, while she agreed with the overall message and spirit of Black Lives Matter (BLM) activists, she was put off by what she saw as the lack of discipline and confrontational approach of its members. In a *USA TODAY* op-ed piece, 2016 GOP presidential candidate Ben Carson made the point that, while he agreed with the BLM stance that racism is indeed a factor in American life, the reality (as he saw it) was that the movement needed to expand its vision and focus its attention on education, the breakdown of the Black family structure, and other factors that he saw as contributing to the disarray plaguing too many lower-income Black communities (Carson, 2015).

What the responses from both of these very accomplished individuals demonstrated is a vast generational divide between older Black baby boomers, millennials, and many Generation Xers in regards to presentation and tactics. Reynolds clearly has memories of the well-dressed, well-behaved, well-spoken protestors (which included a large number of clergy across racial lines and religious faiths) who marched in the South more than a half century ago. These were the men and women who wore their Sunday best to church, as well as on the front lines, as they confronted violent law enforcement and rabid racists and segregationists. Carson assumes that the answer to Black salvation lies in turning off the television, refraining from using profanity, reforming the public school system, cleaner living, and embracing conservative politics.

While likely well intentioned, the fact is that both Reynolds (a liberal) and Carson (a conservative) unwittingly urged young Black activists to subscribe

64

to a form of respectability politics that is likely to do little, if anything, to rectify the pressing issues facing far too many Black youth in the twenty-first century. Throughout history, whenever Black people have adopted the art of civility and decorum toward racism and bigotry, the result has been an upsurge in violence, discrimination, and systematic racism directed toward the larger community. The fact is that violence against Black bodies has always been a part of American life and it is still the case (Sidner, 2015).

We have seen it in the gruesome lynchings of Black men and some women. The violent beatings of Black suspects in police custody. The rapes of Black women at the hands of White men and other forms of physical, sexual, and emotional assault (McGuire, 2014). Particularly disturbing were the brutal rape and beating of Salisa Luster in Louisville, Kentucky (McRae, 2013), the murders of Eugene Ellison and Alvin Allison of Little Rock, Arkansas (Jones, 2014), and Victor White from New Iberia, Louisiana (Illing, 2015). Outside of Black news outlets, local news, and alternative media outlets, hardly any attention was given to these crimes. The same was the case in regards to Monroe Isadore, a 107-year-old man who was shot by a SWAT team in Pine Bluff, Arkansas, in September 2013 (Anon., 2013). Race was a factor in these incidents and these are the sorts of issues that Black Lives Matter is addressing.

The truth is that whenever other groups of people have decided to assert themselves and have the needs of their respective communities addressed, there has been little, if any, resistance or controversial remarks from the larger public. On the contrary, when Black Americans decide to speak truth to power about the crucial issues facing many Black communities, there is an automatic level of resentment, fear, and paranoia from certain segments of society. This is a perverse double standard that is unjust and unfair. Such a reality is evident in the ongoing sinister and viciously dishonest attempts by some members of the conservative right to brand BLM as a hate group as well as attempts to scapegoat the rhetoric of the movement for the high-profile murders of several White police officers. The fact that the majority of White police officers have been murdered at the hands of White people or by individuals or members of White fringe extremist groups seems to have been lost on them. The criticism that emerged from certain segments of the political left was/is that the movement lacks focus, discipline, and should strive to be more sophisticated in its efforts.

Whatever flaws it has (the same can be said about any and all grassroots movements), the fact is that Black Lives Matter activists have expressed their message boldly, clearly, and without apology. The organization is indeed a strong, powerful, and much-needed entity in our current racially tormented and fractured climate.

REFERENCES

Anon. (2013, September 8). SWAT team kills 107-year old Arkansas man in shootout. *CBS News*. Retrieved from https://www.cbsnews.com/news/swat-team-kills-107-year-old-arkansas-man-in-shootout/

Basu, Tanya (2015, August 9). Black Lives Matter activists disrupt Bernie Sanders speech. Retrieved from *Time Magazine*. Retrieved from http://time.com/3989917/black-lives-matter-protest-bernie-sanders-seattle/

Carson, Ben (2015, September 3). Black Lives Matter misfire. *USA Today*. Retrieved from https://eu.usatoday.com/story/opinion/2015/08/24/black-livesmatter-sanders-clinton-anger-column/32055507/

Illing, Sean (2015, August 27). Before Sandra Bland, there was Victor White: Why his death in police custody should have you outraged. *Salon*. Retrieved from https://www.salon.com/2015/08/27/before_sandra_bland_there_was_victor_white_why_his_death_in_police_custody_should_have_you_outraged/

Jones, Joseph (2014, October 23). Eugene Ellison: Little Rock's Michael Brown. *Arkansas Times*. Retrieved from https://www.arktimes.com/arkansas/eugene-ellison-little-rocks-michael-brown/Content?oid=3514149

Lowery, Wesley (2016). *They can't kill us all: The story of the struggle for black lives*. New York, NY: Little, Brown & Company.

Lowery, Wesley (2017, January 17). Black Lives Matter: Birth of a movement. *The Guardian*. Retrieved from https://www.theguardian.com/us-news/2017/jan/17/black-lives-matter-birth-of-a-movement

McGuire, Danielle L. (2014). *At the dark end of the street: Black women, rape and resistance: A new history of the Civil Rights Movement from Rosa Parks to the rise of black power*. Vintage Press.

McRae, Finley F. (2013, September 19). Salisa's story: After brutal rape and police misconduct, a continuing search for justice. *Blackamericaweb.com*. Retrieved from https://blackamericaweb.com/2013/09/19/salisas-story-after-brutal-rape-and-police-misconduct-a-continuing-search-for-justice/

Reynolds, Barbara (2015, August 24). I was a Civil Rights activist in the 1960s, but it's hard for me to get behind Black Lives Matter. *The Washington Post*. Retrieved from https://www.bu.edu/news/2015/08/24/i-was-a-civil-rights-activist-in-the-1960s-but-its-hard-for-me-to-get-behind-black-lives-matter/

Sidner, Sara (2015, December 28). The rise of Black Lives Matter: Trying to break the cycle of violence and silence. *CNN*. Retrieved from https://edition.cnn.com/2015/12/28/us/black-lives-matter-evolution/index.html

Watson, Elwood (2015, September 3). Black Lives Matter movement is shedding light on issues long overlooked or ignored by mainstream society. *Huffington Post*. Retrieved from https://www.huffingtonpost.com/elwood-d-watson/black-lives-matter-moveme_b_8080798.html

14

Black History Month: Beyond One Month

Another year, another February, and we are deep into another Black History Month. As has pretty much always been the case, various institutions and individuals from all walks of life have taken it upon themselves to celebrate the numerous milestones and accomplishments of people of African descent. There was no reason to believe that 2018 would be any different, and it has not. Indeed, it appears to be business as usual as millions of Americans and a few others throughout the world celebrate the history of Black Americans.

For 28 days (some years 29), we will be introduced to and, in some cases, reminded of the innumerable contributions (and rightly so) that Black people have made to this nation. Corporations will make bold and brazen acknowledgments to various Black entertainers, athletes, politicians, educators, ministers, historical figures, and significant facts as they relate to Black America. Black churches and other religious organizations will sponsor dinners (mostly soul food) that represent a culinary smorgasbord of definitive recipes that originated in the African diaspora. Numerous educational institutions from elementary schools to colleges and universities will sponsor a multitude of cultural programs, showcase films and documentaries, bring in various speakers, musicians, poets, and an assorted array of activists of varied stripes as they make every effort to salute Black history. Again, all is good.

The truth is that Black people have a distinct, complex, and vibrant history. This can be said of all ethnic and religious groups. However, the history of Black Americans in this nation is vastly distinct from other ethnic groups due to the religious, economic, social, psychological, and educational experiences that have been visited and inflicted upon us. By exploring and acknowledging Black History Month, the nation is paying homage to a group of men and women who are strong, resilient, innovative, forgiving (in some cases, arguably too forgiving), distinctive, and have contributed immensely to the vitality and success of America. A nation where certain people never intended for us to obtain full citizenship or be fully included within the full panorama of American culture.

In a nation (and sad to say, in some other countries), where Black people are often perennially depicted and showcased as pimps, thugs, prostitutes, derelicts, baby commas, callous welfare recipients, oversexed, and overall retrograde menaces to society (although there has been notable improvement, particularly in regards to commercials over the past few years), Black History Month provides a crucial and vital forum for facts, statistics, distinguished accomplishments, and triumphs that are far too often obscured and dismissed from the public discussion. An opiate of sorts to counter the often negative narratives that are often ascribed to the Black community.

To be fair, racism has always been a part of this nation. It is deeply ingrained in the fabric of our culture and is as American as apple pie. However, what we are seeing now, is blatant and undisguised bigotry of the type that many White people have had to keep disguised since the 1950s or at least since the early 1960s, being unleashed and allowed to unapologetically permeate itself in various sectors of our society, in many cases, without consequences.

Black History Month explores and exposes the ample diversity and plethora of talent that has always existed in the Black community. This diverse exposure dispels the largely held myth by many (particularly White America) that Black America is a one-note monolith (Bolton, 2018).

Our current political and cultural climate virtually necessitates the need for such reinforcement. Anyone who has a pulse and is socially and culturally woke is astute to the current challenges we face in this nation. We have a brazenly racially divisive president who routinely stokes the flames of racial animosity and division and adamantly embraces White supremacists. The time is ripe for a reinforcement of Black excellence to combat the naysayers of such racial resistance (Mitchell, 2018).

Since the time of this nation's inception, we as Black Americans have had to wage a long battle to obtain rights that were supposed to be guaranteed by our constitution, and that most other groups have taken for granted. The mountains and minefields that our ancestors had to climb, face head on and, in many cases, triumphed against, despite enduring seemingly unrelenting adversity is a testament to their impervious strength and spirit. We are enduring similar battles today in the twenty-first century (Reynolds, 2011). Indeed, the fact is that being Black in America often means waging an ongoing battle. It means dealing with a history that has been defined by blood, sweat, tears, pain, occasional dashed dreams, setbacks, and periodic victories.

As I see it, Black history is not some entity that should be confined to one specific month of the year. Such an attitude is disrespectful and patronizing (Ewers, 2018). Rather, the history of Black people (as is the case with the history of other ethnic groups) is one that deserves our full and undivided attention. Food for thought.

REFERENCES

Bolton, Kenna (2018, February 28). Is it time to revisit black history month? *CNN*. Retrieved from https://edition.cnn.com/2018/02/10/opinions/black-history-month-revisited-kerra-bolton-opinion/index.html

Ewers, James (2018, February 11). Honoring black history should go beyond one month. *The Charlotte Post*. Retrieved from http://www.thecharlottepost.com/news/2018/02/11/opinion/honoring-black-history-should-go-beyond-one-month/

Mitchell, Katie (2018, January 27). How to keep black history month and keep celebrating all year long. *Bustle*. Retrieved from https://www.bustle.com/p/how-to-celebrate-black-history-month-2018-keep-celebrating-all-year-long-8003988

Reynolds, Rodney (2011, May 25). Taking black history beyond February. *Huffington Post*. Retrieved from https://www.huffingtonpost.com/rodney-reynolds/taking-black-history-mont_b_488113.html

15

Message to Starbucks: Tackling Racism Will Require More than a Few Hours of Racial Bias Training

On April 12, 2018, two Black men, Rashon Nelson and Donte Robinson were arrested while sitting inside a Starbucks coffeehouse in Philadelphia, Pennsylvania. The men were waiting for a friend/business associate (who was White) to discuss real estate investments. The White female manager on duty, incensed at the fact that the men refused to purchase anything to eat or drink, called the police. Within a matter of minutes, both Nelson and Robinson were handcuffed and escorted out of the building and taken to prison. Both men settled with the city of Philadelphia for $1.00 and with the coffee chain for an undisclosed sum (Siegel, 2018).

Their arrests caused a national outrage and resulted in a public relations fiasco for Starbucks. Then CEO, Kevin Johnson did not help matters with his initial blunders and awkward responses to the situation. He later issued an apology for both his handling of the situation and for the company in general (McGregor, 2018). After a few days, former executive chairman Howard Schultz publicly expressed his embarrassment and met with both men to offer his remorse for the incident that had taken place (Meyer, 2018). A few days later, Schultz announced all Starbucks stores would be closed on May 29th in an effort to train employees about implicit bias (Morris, 2018) and enlisted the rapper Common to assist them with their efforts (Meyer, 2018).

It is important to note that this was not the first time that Starbucks had found itself in the middle of a racial controversy. In March 2015, much of the mainstream media and bloggersphere had been abuzz with frenzied commentary to Starbucks CEO Howard Schultz's efforts to encourage baristas to discuss the issue of race with customers (Wahba, 2015). Reaction ranged from sympathetic and mildly supportive, to cynical, to outright critical (Kaplan, 2015). Personally, I lauded Schultz for taking the initiative to confront an issue (no matter how awkwardly) that has been a perennial, problem in our nation since its inception. However, less than a week later, Starbucks abruptly ended the campaign (Somaiya, 2015).

For many people, race is, indeed, often the 800-pound rambunctious elephant in the room. It is permeating our current state of affairs. The "post-racial" society we supposedly entered with the election of Barack Obama in 2008 was a grand illusion. For the record, in all truthfulness, I (and probably many other people of color) never believed such a fallacy. No person who is attuned to the climate of the current acerbic environment can convincingly argue otherwise; Schultz is to be commended for attempting to tackle this thorny issue.

That being said, the fact is that for far too long any effort to address the issue of race in America has been a largely packaged affair; ceremonial, co-opted, and controlled by well-meaning yet often alarmingly out-of-touch legislators, celebrities, and CEOs. To put it bluntly, many efforts to address the issue of racism in our contemporary culture are often misguided, distressingly adrift, naïve, and tone deaf to the concerns and harsh realities that Black people have to deal with on a daily basis.

Politicians of all races, entertainers, and the occasional athlete, or public intellectual locking arms and singing freedom songs from the civil rights movement more than half a century ago, do little, if anything, to confront the searing issues that are plaguing many communities of color in the twenty-first century.

In fact, over the past several years, numerous department stores such as Macy's, Nordstroms, Abercrombie & Fitch, and others have agreed to pay substantial settlements for racial profiling allegations. And virtually all of us Black folk over 35 years old know all too well of the ongoing saga of being pulled over by law enforcement largely without probable cause — "Driving While Black (DWB)." As you can imagine, there are numerous other examples of the indignities that people of African descent (and many other non-Whites) frequently endure, sometimes on a daily basis.

Having Starbucks baristas serve as goodwill ambassadors leading the nation in addressing the racial problem in our nation was a misguided, yet noble effort that was already dead on arrival (James, 2015). The cold, hard fact is that, at this moment, it is not beneficial for people of color — in particular, Black people — to engage in discussions on race with mainstream (White) America. These sort of "let's come together and talk about it" type of talks do little to solve the problem of systematic and structural racism. Most, if not all of us, are all too aware of racism and its potentially debilitating effect on our lives. Having nice, polite conversations about race have not solved such ills in the past, and there is certainly no reason to believe they will do so now.

The truth is that White Americans will have to come to grips with their racism and begin to have the conversation among themselves. The reason is that many Whites have adopted a defensive posture of White fragility, declaring that things are "not as bad as we think" (D'Angelo, 2015). Rather, on the contrary, we, people of color, are supposedly paranoid, oversensitive, etc. Some hard-line racism deniers actually have the audacity to say that too many of us (Black people) are "ungrateful." Imagine! Having the nerve to ask to be treated fairly in a society that has routinely excluded or, at the very least, marginalized you renders one difficult.

With such polarizing resistance and denial, any attempt at having a fruitful, progressive, and productive discussion on race is likely to be an exercise in futility. It is best, at least for now, that Whites have this most important conversation among themselves. Most Black people, myself included (particularly in this current era of Donald Trump), are suffering from a severe case of racial fatigue and are not willing to go down this dead end road of racial *déjà vu* again anytime soon. Nonetheless, once again, I salute Mr. Schultz for his well-intended, if futile, efforts.

REFERENCES

D'Angelo, Robin (2015, April 9). White fragility: Why it's so hard to talk to white people about racism. *Good Men Project*. Retrieved from https://goodmenproject.com/featured-content/white-fragility-why-its-so-hard-to-talk-to-white-people-about-racism-twlm/

James, Ben (2015, March 31). 5 tips to handle workplace race talks better than Starbucks. *Law 360*. Retrieved from https://www.law360.com/articles/637242/5-tips-to-handle-workplace-race-talks-better-than-starbucks

Kaplan, Sarah (2015, March 17). Starbucks now serving coffee with a dose of debate on race. *The Washington Post*. Retrieved from https://www.washingtonpost.com/news/morning-mix/wp/2015/03/17/starbucks-now-serving-coffee-with-a-dose-of-debate-on-race/?utm_term=.2c50c343607c

McGregor, Jena (2018, April 19). Anatomy of a PR response: How Starbucks is handling it's Philadelphia crisis. *The Washington Post*. Retrieved from washingtonpost.com. https://www.washingtonpost.com/news/on-leadership/wp/2018/04/19/anatomy-of-a-pr-response-how-starbucks-is-handling-its-philadelphia-crisis/?utm_term=.de1ace2ee7aa

Meyer, Zlati (2018, May 29). With "moral courage" Starbucks workers take part in emotional training to avoid racial bias. *USA Today*. Retrieved from https://eu.usatoday.com/story/money/business/2018/05/29/starbucks-howard-schultz-racial-bias-training-discrimination-african- american/652395002/

Morris, David L. (2018, May 26). Starbucks anti-bias training will feature Rapper Common. *Fortune Magazine*. Retrieved from http://fortune.com/2018/05/26/starbucks-anti-bias-training-common/

Obama, Michelle (2016). Speech at the Democratic National Convention. Retreived from https://www.washingtonpost.com/news/post-politics/wp/2016/07/26/transcript-read-michelle-obamas-full-speech-from-the-2016-dnc/?noredirect=on&utm_term=.26a38b94b107

Siegel, Rachel (2018, May 3). Two black men arrested at Starbucks settle with Philadelphia for $1.00 each. *The Washington Post*. Retrieved from washingtonpost.com. https://www.washingtonpost.com/news/business/wp/2018/05/02/african-american-men-arrested-at-starbucks-reach-1-settle-ment-with-the-city-secure-promise-for-200000-grant-program-for-young-entrepreneurs/?utm_term=.a68810467ae6

Somaiya, Ravi (2015, March 22). Starbucks ends conversation starters on race. *New York Times*. Retrieved from https://www.nytimes.com/2015/03/23/business/media/starbucks-ends-tempestuous-initiative-on-race.html

Stevens, Matt (2018, April 15). Starbucks apologizes for arrest of 2 black men. *New York Times*. Retrieved from https://www.nytimes.com/2018/04/15/us/starbucks-philadelphia-black-men-arrest.html

Wahba, Phil (2015, March 16). Starbucks to encourage baristas to discuss race relations with customers. *Fortune Magazine*. Retrieved from https://uk.search.yahoo.com/search?fr=mcafee&type=E211GB978G0&p=Wahba%2C+Phil+(2015%2C+March+16).+Starbucks+to+encourage+baristas+to+discuss+race+ relations+with+customers.

16

We Must Focus More on Substantial Issues as Opposed to Fleeting Symbolism

In June 2015, President Obama delivered a stirring eulogy at the College of Charleston. It was an inspirational speech and a thoughtful reminder on the state of race relations in America. It was during this month that the Rev. Clementa Pinckney, along with eight other church members, were gunned down June 17th of that year by Dylann Storm Roof during Bible study at Emmanuel AME Church, a church with a long and deeply rooted history of Black activism.

One result of this epic tragedy was that many people began to have intense discussions about the Confederate battle flag and other topics that were previously rendered off limits among polite company in the public sphere. Conversation on the issue has primarily focused on the flag's historical legacy, whether it is appropriate for the flag to hang above statehouses and to be sold as merchandise in department stores, on license plates and in other public spheres.

Initial momentum appeared to be on the side of critics who argued that the flag is rooted in a negative legacy and is an affront to a large segment of the American population. A number of Southern states did take the principled and audacious step of removing the flag from their respective statehouse grounds and retiring it to museums. Consumer giant Wal-Mart decided to prohibit selling Confederate merchandise in its stores and other businesses quickly followed suit. One woman, Bree Newsome, took it upon herself to remove the flag by climbing up and removing the flag from the South Carolina state capital in Columbia (Goodman, 2015).

To be sure, there are those supporters who have argued tooth and nail that the flag is merely a part of their heritage and nothing more. The truth is that they need to read up on and develop a more critical comprehension of their American history. Without being too cynical, it is highly unlikely that a number of these previously staunch pro-Confederate propaganda politicians experienced a "road to Damascus" conversion, "turned a corner," and suddenly "saw the light." Rather, the "vision" they saw was the pressure of corporate sponsors and the mood of nationwide public opinion moving in the opposite direction.

While I am well aware of the power and importance of symbols, I also know that symbolic messages alone are not enough. Many times such nominal gestures wind up having insufficient funds when it's time to cash them in. We cannot lose sight of the importance of substance. Over the past few years, various political pockets of the nation have been deeply immersed in passionate (for some opportunistic) debates about flags, what defines marriage, politically correct language, who has the right to use certain words such as nigger, appropriate vs. inappropriate curriculum in high school and college campuses, etc. Such discussions have triggered a wide range of reactions and perhaps some overreactions.

Zero tolerance of all things offensive might lead to advocating banning legendary films such as *Birth of Nation* (1916) and the 1939 Academy Award-winning film *Gone With The Wind*. As a historian, I can attest that this is a bad, quite frankly, foolhardy idea. The truth is that despite the retrograde racist messages that emanate from both films, both works can serve as valuable teaching lessons for younger and future generations by shedding light on a period of America that was very dark, sordid, and far from progressive. The same goes for racial and gender stereotypes such as Aunt Jemima and Uncle Ben, statues named after racists and deconstructing other social issues that have dominated current social discourse.

For the record, I am in agreement with those who believe that the Confederate flag should not be displayed on statehouse grounds and removed from public for many of the aforementioned reasons. Put it in a museum where it belongs and keep it there. Moreover, it would be commendable for Quaker Oats and Mars, Inc. to consider retiring the aunt and uncle labels from their products. Indeed, Jemima's pancakes and Ben's rice will do just fine, thank you.

Passionate discussions aside, it is vital that those of us who desire to see genuine and systematic change do not lose sight of the importance of achieving substantive victories without getting sidetracked by sophistic debates and symbolic gestures. We need to focus on chronically high unemployment in many communities of color (Bertrand, 2016); major health disparities between Blacks and Whites (Randall, 2009); disproportionately high incarceration rates among Black men; discrimination directed toward Black job applicants; violent and aggressive policing in Black and Latino/a communities; and gentrification and housing discrimination.

There are many pressing issues that require our immediate attention and will require a dedicated level of commitment. Making a substantial effort to combat such an unhealthy level of potentially destructive vices that plague our communities as opposed to unwittingly falling prey to embracing fleeting issues should be our primary ongoing and permanent goal.

REFERENCES

Bertrand, Marianne (2016, May 21). The problem has a name: Discrimination. *Chicago Booth Review*. Retrieved from http://review.chicagobooth.edu/behavioral-science/2016/article/problem-has-name-discrimination

DeMille, Oliver (2017, February 27). Symbol vs. Substance. Retrieved from http://oliverdemille.com/symbol-substance/

Goodman, Amy (Interview with Bree Newsome) (2015, July 3). This flag comes down today: Bree Newsome scales SC Capitol flagpole, takes down Confederate flag. *Democracy Now: Independent Global News*.

Randall, Vernilla R. (2009, Fall). Inequality in health care is killing African Americans. *American Bar Association*, 36(11), 123–123.

17

An Open Letter to Some on the Conservative Right: Slavery Was Totally F*cked Up. Period

There are probably a number of people who vaguely remember the remarks made by former FOX News host Bill O'Reilly in regards to First Lady Michelle Obama's speech at the Democratic National Convention in July 2016. For several days, O'Reilly's misguided and pathetic comments downplaying slavery made him the target of ire from a multitude of individuals and citizens from all walks of life. For those unaware of what the first lady said, it was the following:

> I wake up every morning in a house that was built by slaves, and I watch my daughters two beautiful intelligent black young women, playing with their dogs on the White House lawn.

It was evident to anyone with a reasonable degree of comprehension skill that the former first lady was saying: the fact that a person such as herself, the descendant of slaves, is living at the world's most power-laden residence, which also happens to have been built by slave labor, is testament to the opportunities that this nation has and can potentially offer to its citizens, including those who have been historically marginalized and denied opportunities.

On his FOX News program, Bill O'Reilly responded:

> Slaves that worked there were well fed and had decent lodgings provided by the government, which stopped hiring slave labor in 1802. However, the feds did not forbid subcontractors from using slave labor. So Michelle Obama is essentially correct in citing slaves as builders of the White House, but there were others working as well.

It goes on.

Understandably, condemnation was swift. Rather than acknowledge that he missed the point and went far afield, O'Reilly went on the warpath defending his indefensible lunacy, blaming the left-wing media, democratic politicians, his enemies, and all those of political persuasions distinct from his as engaging in intellectual dishonesty (Victor, 2016). You see, it was not his fault that he made such irresponsible comments, it was that his political foes were misrepresenting and distorting his comments. Really? Please!

It was particularly interesting to see the number of Hollywood celebrities that weighed in on the issue. Actress, singer, and Tony Award Winner Audra McDonald, mega TV series producer, Shonda Rhimes, singer Questlove (Hill, 2016), and late night hosts James Corden and Conan O'Brien took the FOX News host to task for his out-of-touch comments (Bradley, 2016). On his July 27th show of that year, Conan O'Brien responded to O'Reilly with a wicked level of wit. "Leave it to FOX News to provide a fair and balanced view of slavery," he said. Ouch! (Hill, 2016).

To be sure, O'Reilly is not the only conservative who has ridiculously and obscenely defended slavery. All one has to do is peruse a number of right-of-center websites — some who identify as conservative as well as others who describe themselves as nationalists — and the ample, rambling level of commentary in support of slavery is astounding. The sad fact is that many of these posters are very likely genuine in their viewpoints. It is galling to witness (Heath, 2014).

O'Reilly's attitude reminded me of the behavior of Scott Terry, an attendee at the Conservative Political Action Committee (CPAC) conference in 2013 who made the case that slavery was not all that bad, but was actually good for Black people, in that it provided them with food, clothing, shelter, and other essentials (Keyes and Beauchamp, 2013). Several of his fellow conference attendees were disgusted by his remarks. Like O'Reilly, Terry's comments drew immediate ire and he eventually backtracked from his callous statements.

It appears that for some on the conservative right, the jury is still out. In October 2017, John Kelly, chief of staff to President Donald Trump argued that the civil war was due to the lack of "ability to compromise." Think about such a statement! (Astor, 2017). The sad fact is that each of these men have plenty of company in regard to their perversely misguided viewpoints (Howard, 2012).

One can only wonder what would make any rational, decent human being assert that slavery was a good thing. The fact is that slavery was violent, responsible for the deaths of millions of people, destroyed families, economically decimated entire populations of people, robbed people of their religion and cultural heritage, and more. There was nothing "positive" about it. This is particularly true in regards to the millions who were lashed down by its cruel and rapacious spirit (Hanlon, 2017). Perhaps White men like O'Reilly, Terry, Kelly – and others who make perverse justifications for slavery as a benign institution – should consider being placed in chains; taken to an unknown territory; being sold to the highest bidder; and then, see how things play out for them.

Better yet, they should take a long, hard look in the mirror of their souls and ask themselves, "Am I defending what I would want for myself?" I can pretty much anticipate what the answer would be.

REFERENCES

Astor, Maggie (2017, October 31). John Kelly pins Civil War on a "lack of ability to compromise". *New York Times.* Retrieved from https://www.nytimes.com/2017/10/31/us/john-kelly-civil-war.html

Bradley, Bill (2016, July 28). James Cordon shuts down Bill O'Reilly's slavery comments. *Huffington Post.* Retrieved from https://www.huffingtonpost.co.uk/entry/james-corden-shuts-down-bill-oreillys-slavery-comments_us_5799f-6d7e4b01180b531d162?guccounter=1&guce_referrer_us=aHR0cHM-6Ly91ay5zZWFyY2gueWFob28uY29tLw&guce_referrer_cs=tePWWuk-w1eWdNgMxgk2ONw

Heath, Terrance (2014, April 30). Can Conservatives stop defending slavery? *OurFuture.org.* Retrieved from https://ourfuture.org/20140430/can-conservatives-stop-defending-slavery

Henlon, Aaron (2017, February 16). Advice for my conservative students. *New York Times.* Retrieved from https://www.nytimes.com/2017/02/16/opinion/advice-for-my-conservative-students.html

Hill, Libby (2016, July 28). Bill O'Reilly courts controversy with comments on slavery: Hollywood hits back. *Los Angeles Times.* Retrieved from https://www.latimes.com/entertainment/gossip/la-et-mg-bill-oreilly-slavery-obama-20160728-snap-htmlstory.html

Howard, Mark (2012, October 23). Ten Conservatives who have praised slavery. *Alternet.* https://www.alternet.org/2012/10/10-conservatives-who-have-praised-american-slavery/

Keyes, Scott, & Beauchamp, Zack (2013, March 15). CPAC participant defends slavery at Minority Outreach Panel: It gave "food and shelter" to blacks. *Think Progress*. Retrieved from https://thinkprogress.org/cpac-participant-defends-slavery-at-minority-outreach-panel-it-gave-food-and-shelter-to-blacks-1959db62fa/

Victor, Daniel (2016, July 27). Bill O'Reilly defends comments about "well fed" slaves. *New York Times*. Retrieved from https://www.nytimes.com/2016/07/28/business/media/bill-oreilly-says-slaves-who-helped-build-white-house-were-well-fed.html

18

Self-Hatred in the Black Community

Anyone who has been meticulously perusing prominent Black websites knows that there is no lack of articles on how many people of color supposedly suffer from poor self-image and a lack of self-esteem. For the longest time, when I came across such material, I pretty much glanced at the title of the article, may have done a quick read, and moved on. After all, I saw myself as someone who was pretty content with myself, and the information and advice being shared in the majority of these articles did not apply to me or the majority of Black people, or at least those Black people who were well educated. Well, a few years ago, this previously misguided assumption on my part ceased when I stumbled across an article written by a fellow person of African descent.

Several years ago, in 2013, I was enamored by an article written by Orville Douglas. Douglas is a Black Canadian journalist who made national and international headlines with his "this is how I really feel" column discussing the self-hatred he had internalized and consumed due to the fact that he is Black (Douglas, 2013). Yes indeed, upon the appearance of his article, the Black blogosphere (and all other avenues of social media) wasted no time dutifully dissecting, critiquing, discussing, and certainly reacting and aggressively responding to Mr. Douglas's article. It appeared that Douglas had engaged in a stroke of public relations genius.

Mild sarcasm aside, no one could deny that his piece punched many Black cultural and political pundits, as well as readers, directly in the face. It was frank, intense, brash, unrelenting, searing, and in many cases gave an insider-perspective on the heartbreaking imprisonment that had gripped this young Black man. It left him with a vehement level of hate, disgust, and resentment, both toward himself and those who share his racial heritage. Some even went so far as to write him an open letter (Cole, 2013). His interview at the time with CNN commentator Don Lemon was candid and engaging. I will admit that when I first read his article, I was stunned. In fact, I had to reread the piece to make sure that my eyesight was not blurred or that my imagination was not running wild. A second thorough read confirmed that what I had previously read was indeed accurate. My sanity was still intact.

I felt myself aching with sympathy for Mr. Douglas. I could almost feel his hurt, isolation, and other forms of distress through his lacerating, "take no prisoners" article. In all honesty, prior to his column, I had never read any piece where a person (in particular, an educated Black person) had been so candid in how so little they thought of themselves. To those of you who were not aware of Mr. Douglas or did not read his piece when it was first published, Douglas discussed his rabid disgust with his physical appearance. He mentioned how he is angry at his "large thick lips" (his description, not mine), broad nose, and being despised by the larger (read White mainstream) world on a daily basis. In fact, he was probably being painfully honest in his remarks.

As someone who grew up with parents who always instilled pride in me and my siblings, I can honestly state that I have never resented the fact that I am Black. Have I ever wondered what it would be like to be a member of another race? Yes I have. I have also thought about how my life would have turned out if I had been born female, or in another nation, or disabled, and other possible scenarios for that matter. However, I have never harbored any self-hatred due to this fact. That being said, I am old enough to realize the cold, hard reality that Douglas' perceptions of himself are not an isolated case.

There is a lot of evidence to suggest that Orville Douglas is far from an aberration. Any astute observer of history is well aware that from the moment Africans arrived on the American shores there was a deliberate effort by some to demean, humiliate, disregard, manipulate, and mistreat people of African ancestry by various extralegal methods. This exercise has taken place for centuries. It should come as no surprise therefore, that such self-hatred is deeply embedded within more than a few of our brethren of all ages.

We can see it in the tests that are given to young Black children involving pictures being shown to them, where far too many see White dolls as prettier (Ahuja, 2009). We saw such self-hatred manifest itself when several Black pro-football players considered a perverse, crude, cruel, loudmouth, misfit, White linebacker named Richie Incognito with a history of disciplinary problems more representative of Blackness than Jonathan Martin — a young, sophisticated, cultured, well-educated, reserved Black man — during the Miami Dolphins saga (Mariotti, 2013). We see it in the plethora of YouTube videos, Twitter hashtags Black-oriented websites, and other venues where a number of Black people are perennially downgrading one another or have something negative to say, about Black men, Black women, Black culture, or Black people in general.

This is further compounded when we routinely see ourselves frequently depicted as drug dealers, prostitutes, lazy, less intelligent, dishonest, shiftless, and in other retrograde images. Such a level of ongoing negativity can certainly take its toll (White, 2016). For much of our history, Black Americans have often been targeted as scapegoats for much that is deficient, dysfunctional, immoral, amoral, or just plain wrong with the world. In many avenues in our society (Jimerson, 2013), Black Americans (in many cases other non-Whites for that matter) are seen as "the other." For the less enlightened, we are people to be objectified, tabloidized, sexualized, racialized, and largely despised. The fact that Douglas is Canadian gave us some insights into the apparent racially regressive attitudes of some of our neighbors north of the border. Perhaps being introduced to positive representations of Black history culture would be a tremendous benefit to him.

One can only hope that during the several years that have passed, Orville Douglas has taken the time to address his personal demons and has taken the journey needed so that he can eventually free himself of such psychological misery sooner rather than later, for the sake of his physical and mental well-being. The undeniable reality (and he obviously knows this) is that he was born Black from the womb, is Black in the present, and will stay Black until the tomb.

REFERENCES

Ahuja, Gitka (2009, March 31). What a doll tells us about race. *ABC News*. Retrieved from https://abcnews.go.com/GMA/story?id=7213714&page=1

Cole III, Charles (2013, November 15). Let's really converse about black self-hatred: A semi open letter to Brother Orville Douglas. *Huffington Post*. Retrieved from https://www.huffingtonpost.com/charles-cole-iii/orville-douglas-black-self-hatred_b_4279216.html

Douglas, Orville L. (2013, October 9). Why I hate being a Black man. *The Guardian*. Retrieved from https://www.theguardian.com/commentisfree/2013/nov/09/i-hate-being-a-black-man

Jimerson, Rufus (2013). *Devaluation, self-hatred, and the effects of underdevelopment on African Americans*. Chicago, IL: Create Space Independent Publishing.

Mariotti, Jay (2013, November 8). How can a black player defend incognito? *Sports Talk Florida*. Retrieved from https://sportstalkflorida.com/nfl/nfl-news/how-can-a-black-player-defend-incognito/

White, Jericha (2016, July 25). Who taught black people to hate themselves? *Odyssey*. Retrieved from https://www.theodysseyonline.com/who-taught-black-people-hate-themselves

19

Rachel Dolezal: The Potential Perversity of White Privilege

In May 2018, Rachel Dolezal (who changed her name to Nkechi Diallo in 2016) was found guilty and charged with perjury and welfare fraud (Haag, 2018). Virtually all segments of the media — liberal, conservative, alternative, mainstream — became deeply immersed in the saga of Rachel Dolezal when the story broke in June 2015. Predictably, social media was knee deep in its commentary on the topic.

Rachel Dolezal was a 37-year-old White woman (according to her birth certificate and biological parents) who identified as Black for more than two decades. Her actual ethnic heritage is German, Czech, Swedish, and Native American. You can't make this stuff up! To paraphrase the old saying, "sometimes the truth is better/stranger than fiction."

When the revelation of her Whiteness became known to the public, Dolezal stepped down as president of the Spokane, Washington, branch of the NAACP and quickly became the target of some not-so-friendly fire from people across the political spectrum. The undisputed truth is that the story was indeed mind boggling. It was as if it had a "Twilight Zone" feel to it. In fact, Spokane, Washington has had a rich and vibrant activist history. Lydia Sims was the first Black woman to lead that city's NAACP chapter. Her son, Ronald Sims, went on to undersecretary in HUD in the Obama administration. In regards to Rachel Dolezal, even after the scandal broke, she made it clear that she considered herself Black despite her ethnic and genetic makeup and has maintained this position ever since.

Those of us who are familiar with Black history or have a solid knowledge of the Black experience are well aware of the fact that there have always been people of color who have engaged in the art of "passing" — choosing to live and identify as White. The reason why certain Black people chose to deny their Black heritage and pass for White was due to the oppression and degradation inflicted and imposed on their siblings, relatives, and fellow brethren by a frequently cruel and inhumane society that refused to acknowledge Black people as human beings. Based on the harsh realities of America's racist history of the time period (particularly pre-1960s America), it was not all that surprising that there were non-White men and women who chose to live as White if they could indeed do so. For some, it was a simple case of survival.

Indeed, American literature is filled with the topic of passing. Both fictionalized and non-fictionalized accounts of the topic from James Weldon Johnson's *The Autobiography of an Ex-Colored Man* (Johnson, 1912); Philip Roth's *The Human Stain* (Roth, 2000); Nella Larsen's *Passing* (Larsen, 1929); Allyson Hobbs' *A Chosen Exile* (Hobbs, 2016); Daniel Scharfstein's *The Invisible Line* (2011); John Howard Griffin's *Black Like Me* (1961); and others approach and explore the subject in deep, varied, intriguing, and compelling ways. The price one often paid for making such a dramatic and drastic decision was that one often had to sever all communication with their family and community. This was one hell of a sacrifice to make.

That being said, what made Dolezal's story atypical was the fact that, rather than attempt to acknowledge that she was part of a race that has historically enjoyed numerous benefits and privileges, she elected to embrace and identify herself with a group of people who have routinely been politically, economically, educationally, and psychologically marginalized by the larger society. This is what has made so many people, myself included, scratch their heads. To be sure, there were some White people who did attempt to pass for Black but they were in the significant minority (Appelbaum, 2015). To those who attempted to do so long before the era of integration, one would have to understandably question their motives (Scharfstein, 2015). Truth be told, attempting to sever ties with your ethnic heritage is always a risky proposition (Cobb, 2015). Moreover, having two biologically White parents, coupled with our now 24/7 advanced media Internet age, it was incredulous and, to a degree, galling for her to believe that she could get away with such deception.

Many people, including her parents, made the case (correctly so) that Dolezal could have made valuable contributions to the NAACP and the Black community in general as a White woman opposed to living under the guise of a Black person. Indeed, a number of civil rights organizations, the NAACP, in particular, have long had considerable White participation and influence. In fact, many of the organizations' early supporters and founders were wealthy, powerful, and influential White and Jewish activists and philanthropists. The same holds true today. Someone who claims to be as supposedly racially curious and astute as Dolezal should have known this.

Being neither a psychologist nor psychotherapist, I will concede that I am unqualified to psychoanalyze Rachel Dolezal. That being said, I will still make the argument that, if her past (and present) behavior is any indication, she obviously is either shamelessly opportunistic or in abject denial. Supporters argued that her demonstrated activism outweighs her actual genetic heritage and that she can be considered as a person who is "transracial" (Le-Breton, 2015). Such a position supports those who argue that race is merely a social as opposed to a biological construct. Her detractors view her as fraudulent, confused, and shameless (Boule, 2015). Still others like William Jelani Cobb provocatively made the case that Dolezal's situation is one that is very complex and not as Black and White as her critics and detractors would like it to appear (Cobb, 2015).

Regardless of what position anyone takes on the issue, the fact is that Rachel Dolezal committed some serious and unethical transgressions regardless of her motives. She claimed to have a father who is Black. She falsely represented herself as part of a culture that she was not part of. She brazenly took advantage of such situations and seemed to have no problem doing so. The fact that Dolezal was able to get away with living as a Black woman, albeit precariously, for so long is ironic as well as troubling.

More telling was the fact that she immediately took to the airwaves brazenly defending her actions. She was able to secure book deals, public speaking gigs, was the subject of a Netflix documentary, and other opportunities that have long eluded working, impressive, dynamic Black women with inspiring stories (Graham, 2015). There is no doubt that a movie adaptation will be down the road. This is a person who, even as she masqueraded as Black, was able to perversely capitalize off her deceptive behavior and could have decided to revert to her authentic and biological White pedigree anytime had she chosen to do so. The truth is that Rachel Dolezal's entire life story is the classic definition of White privilege.

REFERENCES

Appelbaum, Yoni (2015, June 15). Rachel Dolezal and the history of passing for black. *The Atlantic*. Retrieved from https://www.theatlantic.com/politics/archive/2015/06/rachel-dolezal-and-the-history-of-passing-for-black/395882/

Boule, Jamelle (2015, June 12). Is Rachel Dolezal black just because she says she is? *Slate*. Retrieved from https://slate.com/news-and-politics/2015/06/rachel-dolezal-claims-to-be-black-the-naacp-official-was-part-of-the-african-american-community-but-did-she-accept-the-racial-hardships-too.html

Cobb, Jeleni (2015, June 15). Black like her: Rachel Dolezal and our lies about race. *The New Yorker*. Retrieved from https://www.newyorker.com/news/daily-comment/rachel-dolezal-black-like-her

Graham, Renee (2015, June 16). Rachel Dolezal's deception inflicts pain on black women. *Boston Globe*. Retrieved from https://www.bostonglobe.com/opinion/2015/06/16/rachel-dolezal-deception-inflicts-pain-black-women/AsZo3ziPA3dCvErhhzBJ3L/story.html

Griffin, John H. (1961). *Black like me*. New York, NY: Houghton Mifflin.

Haag, Matthew (2018, May 26). Rachel Dolezal who pretended to be black is charged with fraud. *New York Times*. Retrieved from https://www.nytimes.com/2018/05/25/us/rachel-dolezal-welfare-fraud.html

Hobbs, Allyson (2016). *A chosen exile: A history of racial passing in American Life*. Cambridge, MA: Harvard University Press.

Johnson, James W. (1912). *The autobiography of an ex-colored man*. Boston, MA: Sherman, French and Company.

Larsen, Nella (1929). *Passing*. New York, NY: Knopf.

Roth, Philip (2000). *The human stain*. New York, NY: Houghton Mifflin.

Scharfstein, Daniel (2011). *The invisible line: Three American families and the secret journey from black to white*. New York, NY: Penguin Press.

Scharfstein, Daniel (2015, June 15). Rachel Dolezal's *Passing* isn't so unusual. *New York Times*. Retrieved from https://www.nytimes.com/2015/06/25/magazine/rachel-dolezals-passing-isnt-so-unusual.html

Willie-Le-Breton, Sarah (2015, June 16). Why Rachel Dolezal is still welcome among blacks. *The Inquirer*. Retrieved from http://www.philly.com/philly/blogs/thinktank/Among-blacks-former-NAACP-leader-still-welcome.html

20

The Black Community and the Complex Politics of Homophobia

As Kevin Hart's homophobic comments made on social media earlier in his career came to public attention in December 2018, his acerbic remarks reverberated throughout the blogger sphere and beyond. Indeed, things became so tense that the mega comedian who had been tapped to host the 91st annual academy awards eventually forfeited "the role of a lifetime" (Dwyer, 2018) as he described it due to both, intense backlash against his initial comments, and what many people across the political and social spectrum saw as an inadequate level of contrition (Lyons, 2018). The situation became so unhinged that the academy decided to forego having a major host for the 91st annual event (Donnelly, 2019).

In early 2018, MSNBC commentator and political pundit Joy Ann Reid found herself in the middle of a messy, tangled and funky controversy as reports surfaced that for several years in the early to mid 2000's, the esteemed cable host had written a slew of intensely, vehemently homophobic comments attacking select politicians and celebrities she assumed to be gay, as well as gay and lesbian people in general. This same blog had been disabled by 2008. Initial reaction to the news was fierce and immediate. For the record, Reid's blog included inflammatory comments on a number of topics ranging from politics to religion. As was the case with Hart, initial reaction to the news was fierce and immediate.

There were some on the left, progressives in particular, who felt a sense of disappointment and betrayal (Savali, 2018). More than a few people on the conservative right wasted no time in attacking the liberal host (Henry, 2018). The liberal website, *The Daily Beast* placed her column on hiatus (Concha, 2018). The LGBTQ organization, PFLAG National rescinded their annual Straight For Equality in Media award that was scheduled to be awarded to Reid in May 2018 (Zhad, 2018). A number of people across the political spectrum from radio hosts to fellow television pundits urged MSNBC to take aggressive action, with some even demanding that MSNBC terminate Reid.

For her part, Reid issued a public statement arguing that her email account had been "hacked." Not surprisingly, her response raised even more ire among previous skeptics and her diehard detractors. Indeed, there were more than a few eyes rolled and an ample amount of serious shade was thrown at Ms. Reid. In essence, she was given the "negro please!" treatment. After several days, the coverage had become so intense that Reid made a mea culpa on air stating: "I genuinely do not believe that I wrote those hateful things,... but I can certainly understand based on things I have written and tweeted in the past why some people don't believe me." and all but conceded that hackers were not the likely source of her many rancid and scurrilous emails (Wang, 2018).

The fact is that Kevin Hart and Joy Ann Reid and were hardly the first Black people to come under fire for espousing homophobic and anti-Gay comments. On New Year's Eve 2016, gospel singer and evangelist Kim Burrell delivered a scorching denunciation of the LGBTQ community for what she saw as the "perverted and immoral" lifestyle and values that members of gay men and women engaged in. Burrell also threw some drive-by shade on Eddie Long, who at the time of his death was battling cancer. The ultra-conservative Black gospel singer referred to Long as a hypocrite who had disgraced the larger religious community. Long, the late megachurch Atlanta pastor, routinely delivered voraciously blistering sermons denouncing members of the LGBTQ community. Meanwhile he had apparently engaged in homosexual activity in private.

As was the case with Reid, reaction was intense and swift. People from across the entertainment community weighed in on the controversy. Many took Burrell to task for what they saw as her hateful and callous comments (Chandler, 2017). Octavia Spencer, Questlove, Janelle Monáe, Pharrell Williams, Yolanda Adams, Monique, Chaka Khan and others were among those who argued that the statements were unacceptable, uncalled for and had no place in the mindset of people who refer to themselves as Christians (Gore, 2017). Repercussions were swift. In addition to being disinvited from appearing on The Ellen DeGeneres Show at the time, Burrell's own radio show — Bridging the Gap — was cancelled (*Ebony*, 2017).

Interestingly, Shirley Caesar, the godmother of female gospel singers, was one the few public figures who rallied to the defense of the embattled singer (Whiteside, 2017).

There was a similar case with former *Grey's Anatomy* actor, Isaiah Washington, who found himself in an intense situation that spiraled out of control and eventually cost him his role as Dr. Preston Burke on the ABC hit drama *Grey's Anatomy* in 2007 (Fleeman, 2007) when it was revealed that he had made disparaging comments about fellow openly gay cast member, T.R. Knight. He eventually returned to the series in 2014. In late January 2019, D.L. Hughley and Terry Crews had a tense back and forth about Crews not reacting aggressively enough to what was seen as a homosexual gesture by former WWE talent agent, Adam Venit (Scott, 2019).

In Burrell's case, the Black bloggersphere was awash in posts on the subject, with many employing quotes from the Bible as they came to the defense of Burrell while many others decried what they saw as her ignorance and insensitivity. For her part, Burrell stood her ground, refused to apologize, and argued that her words had been "misconstrued" and taken out of context (Lang, 2017). Each of the aforementioned individuals added their undeniably controversial perspectives on an issue that has been an ongoing source of contention within the Black community—homophobia. The truth is that homophobia has been problematic within the Black community for decades, arguably centuries.

This is nothing new. The fact is that many Black Americans have always been socially and culturally conservative, especially when it comes to issues of reproductive rights and sexuality in general. This has been due to the deep religious focus that has been so important within much of the Black community from the days of slavery to the present. For centuries, more than a few Black pastors have railed against what they see as the supposed "retrograde" value system and behavior associated with homosexuality and lesbianism. In fact, it is probably rare to find a Black person in their mid 30s or older who has attended church on a regular basis and not heard the pastor in question make blunt, if not outright, virulent comments about gay people.

Terms such as "immoral", "sinful", "perverted", and "unchristian" are just a few of the likely words to come roaring out of his or her mouth. The book of Leviticus gets referred to, dissected and recited in depth (often selectively) by those who want to deride and belittle others (Johnson, 2012). To be sure, there are Black pastors that have taken a minimal or even neutral stance on the issue. However, they are few and far between.

Indeed, it was not uncommon for mid-twentieth-century pastors such as Adam Clayton Powell and other Black ministers of the era to levy unflattering comments and brutal attacks attacks on gays and lesbians. In fact, those Black men and women who were found to be gay or were openly gay were often marginalized, ostracized and viewed with a critical, suspicious or jaundiced eye from many, if not most, members of the congregation and the larger Black community in general. It was/is not uncommon for a number of Black LGBTQ men and women to be subjected to routine, occasionally psychological, and in some cases physical, violence from their communities. At the very least, they have faced considerable levels of marginalization.

Bayard Rustin, the brilliant, skilled organizer and primary brainchild behind the legendary 1963 March on Washington was all but sidelined form the festivities of that day given his open sexuality and refusal to conceal it. Even Martin Luther King Jr. who respected Rustin's organizational acumen, was forced to maintain his distance from his fellow human rights advocate because of Rustin's sexuality (Thrasher, 2013). Truth be told, the Civil Rights Movement, like many avenues of Black America (and America in general at the time), was rife with homophobia. Even today, more than half a century later, many young Black gays and lesbian people are ignored, shamed or dismissed in their communities by their elders, and in some cases even by their younger cohorts.

The fact is that large segments of our community harbor deep and passionate viewpoints on gay and lesbians. At barbershops, beauty shops, on the basketball court, at grandma's house on the holidays with anti-gay relatives, and other places where Black folk tend to congregate, the topic of homosexuality is bound to come up. More often than not, the sentiment — particularly among Black people, let's say, aged over 45 — is negative, or at the very least, ambivalent.

For myself, such a mindset is interesting, perplexing and arguably hypocritical, given the fact that Black gays and lesbians have made significant contributions to the Black community, especially in the Black church and beyond. In fact, it used to be common narrative among certain Black folk that, if it were not for heterosexual Black women and gay Black men, the churches would have been extinct a long time ago. From the choir director, choir members, piano player, ushers, congregation members, and, in some cases, the pastor himself or herself, gays and lesbians have always been actively involved in the religious community, even if not always visible (Harriot, 2017). Something tells me that Kim Burrell and many others know this to be the case.

Religious mores and customs aside, from James Baldwin, Audre Lorde, Bayard Rustin, Lorraine Hansberry, Nella Larsen, George Washington Carver, Zora Neale Hurston, Alain Locke, Josephine Baker, Langston Hughes, June Jordan, James Cleveland, Octavia Butler, Jean Toomer, Barbara Jordan and many others who are still alive, the LGBTQ community has been an integral and vibrant part of the Black community. Imagine the void that would be left in the Black intellectual and cultural sphere without several or all of the aforementioned individuals! In fact, as quiet as it is kept, the reason why certain segments of the Black community have been either reluctant or outright refused to support the Black Lives Matter movement is due to the sexuality of several of its founding members, several of whom are either gay or bisexual, including Deray McKeeson and Alicia Garza among others.

While not as pronounced as it has been in the past, especially among Black millennials, the perception among many Black people is that homosexuality is largely a "White people's thing" and that the supposedly few Black people who do embrace or engage in such a lifestyle are freaks, social deviants, or emulating the White man or woman.

Given the intense hostility that more than often is unleashed among them, many Black LGBTQ men and women decide to suffer in silence. Thus, due to such denial and, in some cases, outright hypocrisy in segments of our various communities, we have seen enormously troubling rates of HIV, AIDS and other venereal diseases horrifically ravage parts of our community. This is due to the fact that so many of our brothers and sisters who fall into this category do not feel that they can be their true selves. Thus, they have to live a life filled with hypocrisy and facades, participating in sham marriages, sheltering, disguising and obscuring their sexuality in secret shadows or on the down-low, and in some cases denouncing themselves and living in a quandary of self-hatred.

Recent studies indicate that Black Americans are no more homophobic than any other group of people. That being said, for many in the Black community (though certainly not all, especially among millennials and centennials) our attitudes and dispositions toward sex in general is draconian, antiquated, outmoded, and, in some cases, is even killing us. Homophobia as well as sexuality is an issue that Black America has to acknowledge, get woke about and come to grips with. We must keep it real and begin to speak truth to power with unabashed candor. Our potential survival and ability to move forward as a people may depend on being able to do so.

REFERENCES

Anon. (2017), Kim Burrell loses show after anti-gay comments. *Ebony*. Retrieved from https://www.ebony.com/entertainment/kim-burrell-radio-show/

Chandler, D.L. (2017). Stars speak out condemning Kim Burrell's homophobic sermon. *Hip Hop Wired*. Retrieved from https://hiphopwired.com/531139/kim-burrell-celebrities-react/

Concha, Joe, (2018, April 26). Daily Beast to hit pause on Joy Reid columns; MSNBC host backs out of speaking event. *The Hill*. Retrieved from https://thehill.com/homenews/media/384979-daily-beast-to-hit-pause-on-joy-reid-columns-msnbc-host-backs-of-speaking

Donnelly, Matt. (2019 , January 9). After Kevin Hart debacle, Oscars forge ahead hostles. *Variety*. Retrieved from https://variety.com/2019/film/news/oscars-no-host-2019-kevin-hart-1203103010/#!

Dwyer, Colin. (2019, December 7). Kevin Hart bows out as Oscar host amid backlash over past tweets. *NPR News*. Retrieved from https://www.npr.org/2018/12/07/674447464/kevin-hart-bows-out-as-oscars-host-amid-backlash-over-past-tweets/?t=1551094029917

Fleeman, Mike (2007, July 2). Isaiah Washington explains why he used slur. *People*. Retrieved from https://people.com/celebrity/isaiah-washington-explains-why-he-used-slur/

Gore, Sydney (2017, January 2017). Kim Burrell is receiving major backlash for her homophobic comments. *Nylon*. Retrieved from https://nylon.com/articles/kim-burrell-homophobic-comments

Harriot, Michael (2017, January 2017), Stop pretending to be shocked at homophobia in the black community. *The Root*. Retrieved from https://www.theroot.com/stop-pretending-to-be-shocked-at-homophobia-in-the-blac-1792228332

Henry, Warren (2018, June 5). Why MSNBC won't fire Joy Reid even though she's a liar. *The Federalist*. Retrieved from http://thefederalist.com/2018/06/04/msnbc-doesnt-fire-joy-reid-even-though-obvious-shes-liar/

Hicks, Tony (2017, January 5). Ellen DeGeneres and Pharrell talk Kim Burrell controversy. *The Mercury News*. Retrieved from https://www.mercurynews.com/2017/01/05/ellen-degeneres-and-pharrell-explain-kim-burrell-controversy/

Jackson, Charreah K. (2017, January 18). 'The death of Bishop Eddie Long and the reckoning of the black church. *Essence*. Retrieved from https://www.essence.com/culture/death-bishop-eddie-long-and-reckoning-black-church/

Johnson, A. (2012, May 12). The historic roots of homophobia in Black America. *The Grio*. Retrieved from https://thegrio.com/2012/05/21/the-historic-roots-of-homophobia-in-black-america/

Lang, Cody (2017, January 3). Gospel singer Kim Burrell addresses backlash after homophobic remarks. *Time Magazine*. Retrieved from http://time.com/4620832/kim-burrell-homophobic-comments/

Lyons, Kate (2018, December 7). Kevin Hart steps down as Oscar host after three days of controversy. *The Guardian*. Retrieved from https://www.theguardian.com/film/2018/dec/07/kevin-hart-steps-down-as-oscars-host-after-three-days-of-controversy

Reynolds, Daniel (2016, May 26). Why can't we talk about homophobia in the black community? *The Advocate*. Retrieved from https://www.advocate.com/politics/2015/05/26/why-cant-we-talk-about-homophobia-black-community

Savali, Kirsten West (2018, June 2). Joy Ann Reid apologizes for blog posts... again. *The Root*. https://www.theroot.com/joy-ann-reid-apologizes-for-blog-posts-again-1826503886

Scott, Katie. (2019, January 28). Terry Crews confronts DL Hughley for mocking his sexual assault case. *Global News*. Retrieved from https://globalnews.ca/news/4897328/terry-crews-dl-hughley-sexual-assault/

Thrasher, Steven (2013, August 27). Bayard Rustin: The man homophobia almost erased from history. *Buzzfeed*. Retrieved from https://www.buzzfeed.com/steventhrasher/walter-naegle-partner-of-the-late-bayard-rustin-talks-about

Wang, Amy B. (2018, April 28). Joy Reid apologizes for anti-LGBTQ posts says she can't prove her blog was hacked. *Washington Post*.

Whiteside, Jude (2017, January 5). Pastor Shirley Caesar comments on the Kim Burrell backlash. *The Shade Room*. Retrieved from http://theshaderoom.com/pastor-shirley-caesar-comments-on-the-kim-burrell-backlash/

Zhao, Christina (2018, April 25). Joy Reid's new homophobic blog post vomments prompt LGBTQ group to take back award. *Newsweek*. Retrieved from https://www.newsweek.com/lgbt-group-rescinds-joy-reids-award-after-homophobic-blog-posts-revealed-900071

21

Michael Dyson and Cornel West: Much Ado about Ego

Most Americans remember how large segments of the Black bloggersphere, in particular, Black Twitter, as well as many in higher education, went deep into overtime in response to the lengthy essay written by Professor Michael Eric Dyson that heavily criticized his fellow Black intellectual academic brother, Professor Cornel West in April 2015 (McLemee, 2015). In all frankness, criticizing is too mild a word. Dyson's article was a searing takedown of West and of what he saw was as the "irrational, immature, petty" and otherwise less than positive attitude that West had exhibited toward him, President Obama, other leading Black intellectuals, and aspects of Black intellectual culture in general (Dyson, 2015).

A number of observers characterized the feud between Dyson and West as a boxing match, battle of the narcissists, petty opportunism at its worst, and other derisive terms (Zirin, 2015). This sort of animated speculation and voyeurism is problematic for a number of reasons. First, it assumes a certain degree of clairvoyant ability that none of us possess. The fact is that only Dyson and West know what motives and emotions lie in their hearts and agendas. For all of those who were captivated by the feud between two prominent members of the contemporary Black intelligentsia, the fact is that such behavior is far from odd. In fact, it is pretty normal.

In my experience dissent among the Black intellectual elite is nothing new. Indeed, writers, politicians, community activists, entertainers, professors, ministers, and others have publicly sparred with one another for centuries. Examples of this are:

- Booker T. Washington and WEB DuBois
- WEB DuBois and Marcus Garvey

- Marcus Garvey and the Black leadership class of the early twentieth century
- Richard Wright and Zora Neale Hurston
- Richard Wright and James Baldwin
- Malcolm X and the Black leadership class of the mid-twentieth century
- Martin Luther King and Whitney Young
- SCLC and CORE

Black folks hurling verbal grenades in public is a past-time as old as the republic itself (Love, 2015). Charges of narcissism, opportunism, confusion, and self-promotion were routinely attributed to one another. Many of these public activists, entertainers, and intellectuals (then as well as now) made the case that their often critical and frequently acerbic commentary was due to their love and concern for the people (larger Black community). Indeed, many of these individuals would often further make the case that they were criticizing one another from a place of constructive yet needed criticism. West made this point in his brutal criticism of former President Obama during his tenure as president. Dyson resorted to this position in his very public verbal dress down of West.

There are those who argue that Black folk publicly disagreeing with one another is problematic, unproductive, only serves as an amusing spectacle to White bigots and does a great disservice to the larger Black community who have more pressing issues that need to be addressed (Younge, 2015). I would take the position that those who dislike and outright despise Black people (and there are quite a few people who do) are going to keep on reveling in their hate regardless of whether we decide to take on one another. They have never had our best interests at heart, nor any of our interests for that matter, and it would be an exercise in gross futility to be concerned about their largely indifferent opinions.

The point is that disagreements and acute public attacks between Black folks are legendary. While it is important to remember that we are all human and none of us are above criticism, it is also crucial that we make an effort to criticize one another in a manner that is constructive in nature as opposed to engaging in mean-spirited, petty, paranoid diatribes that primarily only serve to soothe bruised and tortured egos. We should keep this perspective in mind as we move further into the twenty-first century.

REFERENCES

Dyson, Michael E. (2015, April 19). The ghost of Cornel West: What happened to America's most exciting black scholar? *The New Republic*. Retrieved from https://newrepublic.com/article/121550/cornel-wests-rise-fall-our-most-exciting-black-scholar-ghost

Love, David A. (2015, April 21). Dyson vs. West: Black "Leaders" have never agreed on everything—and that's OK. *The Grio*. Retrieved from https://thegrio.com/2015/04/21/dyson-cornel-west-black-intellectuals/

McLemee, Scott (2015, April 22). Decline of the West II: The Dysoning. *Inside Higher Ed*. Retrieved from https://www.insidehighered.com/views/2015/04/22/commentary-dispute-between-michael-eric-dyson-and-cornel-west

Younge, Gary (2015, April 20). The Cornel West–Michael Eric Dyson feud: Black people are dying in the streets. *The Guardian*. Retrieved from https://www.theguardian.com/commentisfree/2015/apr/20/cornel-west-michael-eric-dyson-feud-petty-black-people-dying

Zirin, Dave (2015, April 20). Cornel West is not Mike Tyson. *The Nation*. Retrieved from https://www.thenation.com/article/cornel-west-not-mike-tyson/

22

1-800-Blame-A-Black-Man

In 1994, legendary comic (arguably the emperor of Black comedians) Paul Mooney, produced a comedic CD titled *Race*, considered a classic by many critics. The album was a bitter, unrelenting screed on America's racial climate during the mid-1990s. One particular segment on the album was entitled "1-900-Blame A Nigger." This was a response to several situations in which White people falsely accused Black people of committing crimes. While ferociously funny and satirically amusing, it was a brutally honest take on the friction, complexities, and fragmentation of the nation's racial history. Almost a quarter of a century later, it seems that little has changed on this front.

In March 2017, an 18-year-old White woman from Denison, Texas, Breana Talbott, was arrested and charged with a Class B misdemeanor for making a false report of being kidnapped and raped (Andrews, 2017). While lying about rape (a serious act of human violation) in and of itself is despicable, the fact is that Talbott did not stop there. Her lies got even more detailed. She brazenly stated that she was raped and assaulted by three Black men, and that was just the beginning. The obviously disturbed teen inflicted wounds upon herself and had the audacity to run to a local church half-naked in a shirt, bra and underwear, screaming to the congregation that she had been raped and assaulted. Upon reading this I thought, Lord, have mercy on this wayward heathen's soul.

This galling act of dishonesty prompted Black Twitter and various social media to call out Talbott and tell her about her dangerously wayward, sorry, racial-profiling self. Interestingly, though not surprisingly, the amount of traffic on many right-wing websites as it related to the real story became notably muted after the fact. Such cricket sounding activity was in stark contrast to the previous week when *The Daily Stormer, Stormfront,* and other alt-right and far-right blogs and websites engaged in all sort of standard racial invective in denouncing the supposed Black male perpetrators. Terms such as monkeys, apes, thugs, beasts, etc. dominated the discourse. Reality had these bigoted derelicts running for cover as they cut tail and ran from what was obviously a falsehood. The truth and reality of what actually transpired did not fit standard right-of-center or far-right, White supremacist narrative. The truth as they often/always see it.

The Denison, Texas Police Department posted a lengthy response to the unfortunate situation (Burch, 2017). What was notable in the statement was the fact that police were apparently suspect of Talbott from the outset. Her story seemed to unravel rapidly day by day as the investigation progressed. The Denison Police Department was understandably furious that numerous resources were diverted and now, wasted, and other real criminal investigations were put on hold in an effort to solve supposed crime where there was, in fact, none. Talbot was indicted on felony charges in July 2017 (Edwards, 2017).

The citizens of Denison, and in particular, communities of color, were enraged and rightly so. That being said, it was more important that some innocent Black men were not unfairly prosecuted and imprisoned due to the fabricated story of some attention-seeking teenage White girl. Justice, despite the resentment that accompanied it, prevailed in this particular case.

Throughout much of American history, one of the most effective ways for a White person who had misbehaved or committed a crime to evade accountability was to scapegoat a Black person as the culprit. We have seen this sort of behavior manifest itself repeatedly. Two grossly perverse examples of this typical "the Black man did it" defense were witnessed in the cases of Charles Stuart and Susan Smith. In the fall of 1989, Charles Stuart, a 29-year-old White man, brutally murdered his wife in cold blood, shot himself in the abdomen, and dialed 911 to report that a "raspy-voiced Black man" had shot him and his pregnant wife and then left them both for dead (Naughton, 1990).

A few years later, in 1994, Susan Smith allowed her car to roll into a lake in Union, South Carolina, to drown her two young sons. She then went on national television tearfully crying "mommy loves you" to her by now dead sons and wickedly pointed the finger at the mythical Black man "wearing a ski mask" who supposedly robbed her, forced her out of her car, and drove off with her two children. Needless to say, she lied (Bragg, 1995). Both cases drew intense media attention. Racial tensions engulfed both Black and White communities.

In Stuart's case, a Black man named Willie Bennett was falsely charged with the crime. After several weeks and a confession brought forward by Stuart's own brother to Boston police, Stuart jumped to his death from a Boston bridge as police closed in on him. Were it not for the albeit reluctant, yet admirable behavior of a sibling, Willie Bennett may very well be sitting in jail more than two decades later. In fact, some observers have argued that decades later, Boston is still reeling from the aftershocks of this event (Scalese, 2014). Meanwhile, in Smith's case, due to clever and skillful techniques of small-town law enforcement officials, she cracked under pressure and admitted to murdering her two children (Anon., 1994).

What these two chilling examples provided is proof of the alarming vulnerability of Black people (particularly Black men) to such irresponsible behavior. To be sure, there have been Black and other non-White individuals who have concocted fabricated falsehoods and hoaxes against other people, and they have, for the most part, been roundly and appropriately condemned and, in a number of cases, prosecuted for their irresponsible actions. No race of people have a monopoly on devious or deviant behavior. That being said, when it comes to being accused of crimes, Black people, in particular Black men, more often than not are usually denied the benefit of the doubt and, rather, are routinely seen as "guilty until proven innocent."

Such attitudes and policy are the products of a nation deeply rooted in historical, racial animus (Young, 2016). Hell, even Charles Manson, the deviant White supremacist and psychopathic murderer who died in November 2017, was astute enough to the racial history of our nation (in a perverse manner) to concoct a gruesome, sadistic crime where he assumed that law enforcement and the public would be gullible enough to believe that Black men (in this case, the Black Panthers) murdered several wealthy Hollywood celebrities as he carried out his atrocious, paranoid fantasy of a race war, without success (Gilbert, 2017).

The fact is that old habits are hard to break. Nonetheless, we as a supposedly ongoing and evolving society must make a valiant effort to rectify such racially reductive attitudes. Such dispositions have no place in twenty-first-century America.

REFERENCES

Andrews, Travis M. (2017, March 23). "Hoax": Texas teen made up widely publicized story of being kidnapped, raped by 3 black men, police say. *Washington Post*. Retrieved from https://www.washingtonpost.com/news/morning-mix/wp/2017/03/23/hoax-texas-teen-made-up-widely-publicized-story-that-3-black-men-kidnapped-and-gang-raped-her-police-say/?utm_term=.c1518c8fd401

Anon. (1994, November 7). Susan Smith's confession. *Time Magazine*. Retrieved from http://content.time.com/time/nation/article/0,8599,2240,00.html

Bragg, Rich (1995, August 4). A killer's only confidant: The man who caught Susan Smith. *New York Times*. Retrieved from https://www.nytimes.com/1995/08/04/us/a-killer-s-only-confidant-the-man-who-caught-susan-smith.html?mtrref=www.google.com&gwh=F720DDE40FB020936C9B-FAB3012A9CFA&gwt=pay

Burch, Chief Jay/Denison Texas Police Department (2017). Date of release: March 22, 2017. Facebook.

Edwards, Breena (2017, July 27). White woman who lied about being kidnapped raped by 3 black men indicted on felony charges. *The Root*. Retrieved from https://www.theroot.com/white-woman-who-lied-about-being-kidnapped-raped-by-3-1797302783

Gilbert, David (2017, November 20). Murderous cultist Charles Manson dies having failed to inspire a race war. *Vice News*. Retrieved from https://news.vice.com/en_us/article/9kddxe/murderous-cultist-charles-manson-dies-having-failed-to-inspire-a-race-war

Naughton, Jim (1990, January 8). The murder that ravaged Boston. *Washington Post*.

Scalese, Roberto (2014, October 22). The Charles Stuart murders and the racist branding Boston just can't seem to shake. *Boston Herald*. Retrieved from https://www.boston.com/news/local-news/2014/10/22/the-charles-stuart-murders-and-the-racist-branding-boston-just-cant-seem-to-shake

Young, Daniella (2016, August 19). White lies: A brief history of white people lying about crimes. *The Root*. Retrieved from https://www.theroot.com/white-lies-a-brief-history-of-white-people-lying-about-1790856437

23

Does Black America Deserve Reparations? Yes. Period

For the past three decades, the issue of reparations has ebbed and flowed in the American psyche. The subject began to gain steam in the early 1990s during the Clinton administration when many activists believed that Clinton's centrist/liberal politics lent itself to a political climate that was conducive to, at the very least, exploring such a possibility.

Like anything in America that involves race, the issue immediately garnered passionate supporters and equally ardent detractors. Many of these supporters and critics drew lines in the sand and quickly retreated to ideological corners. The public was saturated with the predictable "reparations are deserved because..." (Boule, 2014), "Reparations would be problematic and unjust due to the fact that..." (Horrocks, 2016), and so on.

The truth was that each side was so busy in trying to aggressively maneuver and stealthily outwit one another that the occasional thoughtful and reflective arguments that sporadically emerged from the blasting fireworks and snarky rhetoric were quickly dismissed as "idealistic but impractical." This was a less brutal way of saying to your opponents that you made some good points, but I still disagree with you.

Reparations briefly resurfaced during the Obama presidency. Not surprisingly, there were more than a few people who thought, perhaps condescendingly and naively, given the fact that a Black man was finally commander-in-chief, that the issue would be given ample support. However, such optimism rapidly faded as Obama made it clear of his opposition to reparations (at least in the manner that they were being discussed at the time). Such a blatant rejection by the former president caused a degree of demoralization among progressive activists and the subject was quickly relegated to the back burner of priorities and replaced by more largely young, White, liberal, educated, millennial identified causes such as occupy wall street, environmental issues, LGBTQ rights, etc.

Ta-Nehishi Coates' seminal article "The Case for Reparations," which appeared in the June 2014 issue of *The Atlantic Monthly*, once again rebounded the issue front and center into the public sphere (Coates, 2014). While a few new voices were raised and additional arguments were made, most of the rhetoric was merely more rehashed commentary from earlier decades. Virtually no fresh or provocative messages were to be heard. After little more than a year, the issue, once again, went underground. It was business as usual.

Now, as another presidential election approaches, the topic has regained traction among many democratic candidates. A number of 2020 hopefuls have avidly embraced the subject with their own ideas of how such a policy would be implemented as they call for discussions on the matter (Herndon, 2019).

While some Black people and White progressives turn a hopeful ear to such messages, there are those of us (include me in this category) who are less than enthusiastic about what we are hearing. We are what some would refer to as the cynics. Yes, we are the racially conscientious men and women who sigh and give the side eye (Hutchinson, 2019). After so many promising starts routinely followed by abrupt and sudden stops, we cannot help but echo "oh Lord, here we go again, how long will it last this time?"

Cynicism aside, I, like many others, genuinely want to see reparations given full, serious attention and deep consideration and not just at various junctures for disingenuous politicians to exploit for opportunistic purposes (Shipp, 2019). The subject is too crucial to be mishandled and manipulated. Sad to say, up until now this has been the case.

To all those who argue that the issue needs to be debated, I say what is there to debate? The question as to whether people of African descent past or present deserve to be compensated for past and present injustices should not be "up for discussion." We already know the answer. It is a resounding yes. (Watson, 2019).

This nation has financially awarded various groups such as Japanese Americans, Holocaust survivors, and other groups (as they very well should have) for their pain, humiliation, and intense suffering. Goodness knows if there is any group in America that deserves recompense for the numerous iniquities, indignities, and injustices mentally inflicted upon them, it is Black Americans (Austin, 2013).

The Black experience in America is a distinctive one that has been simultaneously marked and marred with rivers of blood, mountains of sweat, and more than a few tears. Such historical and sadistic treatment has consistently manifested itself centuries later in various and menacing ways:

- Rampant abject poverty
- Subpar educational performance
- Hyper segregated school systems with grossly inadequate funding
- Chronic obesity levels due to lack of access to quality food in many Black neighborhoods
- Staggeringly high HIV rates
- Drug epidemic in many Black communities (the same can be said for a growing number of lower income and working-class White communities as well)
- Disproportionate numbers of Black men in prison compared to the general population
- Inadequate living conditions in many Black neighborhoods
- Intense levels of violence due to poverty and lack of economic opportunities
- Rampant police brutality
- Environmental racism
- Poor high-school graduation rates
- Low college graduation rates
- Hyper segregated communities
- High levels of mental health issues
- Systemic and systematic racism and discrimination in virtually all areas of life

The list goes on. No reasonable person can deny these indisputable truths. Most, if not all, of the aforementioned vices are largely due to centuries of past and present circumstances that afflict many people of African descent (Craven, 2016). The psychological impact is real.

To all those Whites people who make the argument that they did not enslave anyone or that they and their relatives never owned slaves, we should respond that this entirely misses the point. The truth is that White people have benefited from past and present retrograde institutional policies that had, and still have, a disproportionate negative impact on many Black people.

Discussions on how such reparation policies would be implemented are ones that are ripe for thoughtful, engaging, and robust debate. Some ideas I would suggest are:

- First time home buyer programs (Collins, 2017)
- Free public and private education or total student loan forgiveness
- Aggressive affirmative action programs
- Addressing the massive White/Black wealth gap (Smith, 2019)
- A Marshall plan for our impoverished urban areas
- Free pre-school programs
- Mandatory education programs on the history of Black Americans and other indigenous people etc.

These would be just some of my recommendations. These would primarily be geared toward middle-aged and younger Black people. Black people who have reached a certain age, say 65 or older, should be allowed to be issued direct monetary compensation. They have lived under what would be considered horrendous levels of humiliation. Moreover, the clock is ticking for these men and women and Father Time will likely be visiting sooner rather than later.

America likes to pride itself on being a fair and just society embedded with the ideas of freedom and justice for all. In the case of many Black Americans, it has fallen woefully and distressingly short. I can think of no better way to make amends by paying a debt that is long overdue.

REFERENCES

Austin, Michael A. (2013, February 1). Reparations for slavery: Why the U.S. government should pay slave reparations. *Psychology Today*. Retrieved from https://www.psychologytoday.com/us/blog/ethics-everyone/201302/reparations-slavery

Boule, Jamelle (2014, May 22). Reparations are owed: Here are a few ways to pay the bill. *Slate.com*. Retrieved from https://slate.com/news-and-politics/2014/05/reparations-should-be-paid-to-black-americans-here-is-how-america-should-pay.html

Coates, Ta-Nehishi (2014, June). The case for reparations. *The Atlantic Monthly*. Retrieved from https://www.theatlantic.com/magazine/archive/2014/06/the-case-for-reparations/361631/

Collins, Chuck (2017, June 23). This is what reparations could actually look like in America. *Quartz.com*. Retrieved from https://qz.com/1012692/this-is-what-reparations-could-actually-look-like-in-america/

Craven, Julia (2016, February 23). We absolutely could give reparations to Black people: Here's how. *Huffington Post*. Retrieved from https://www.huffington-post.co.uk/entry/reparations-black-americans-slavery_n_56c4dfa9e4b08ffac1276bd7

Herndon, Astead (2019, February 21). 2020 Democrats embrace race-conscious policies, including reparations. *New York Times*. Retrieved from https://www.nytimes.com/2019/02/21/us/politics/2020-democrats-race-policy.html

Horrocks, Leann (2016, February 15). Black only reparations?: Good luck. *American Thinker*. Retrieved from https://www.americanthinker.com/articles/2019/02/blackonly_reparations_good_luck.html

Hutchinson, Earl O. (2019, March 12). Ten reasons why the Pesky issue of reparations won't go away. *The Hutchinson Report*. Retrieved from http://www.thehutchinsonreport.net/ten-reasons-why-the-pesky-issue-of-reparations-wont-go-away/

Shipp, E. R. (2019, April 16). Reparations should be more than a throwaway campaign pledge. *Baltimore Sun*. Retrieved from https://www.baltimoresun.com/news/opinion/oped/bs-ed-op-0417-shipp-reparations-20190416-story.html

Watson, Elwood (2019, May 5). Does Black America deserve reparations? Yes! Period! *Medium.com*. Retrieved from https://medium.com/@elwoodwatson890/does-black-america-deserve-reparations-yes-period-730043401bcf

PART III

Physical and Psychological Violence against Black Bodies

24

Violence against and
Demonization of Black Women
Is Often Overlooked

During the summer of 2014, various media outlets replayed the horrifically shocking video of a medium-sized Black woman, Marlene Pinnoch, a homeless woman and grandmother, being brutally pummeled in the face by a physically large California Highway Patrol officer. Such a horrific image sent shock waves as well as outrage through many communities in America. The officer Daniel Andrew was placed on paid leave but eventually exonerated for his actions (Anon, 2015).

In response to the massive public outcry after the video's release to the public, CHP officials responded that they were "investigating" the situation. Really?! Wow! I guess this was a step up from their (CHP) initial response, which was to ignore the case despite the fact that the beating took place in broad daylight with hundreds of drivers and a few onlookers witnessing such a horrendous spectacle. The fact is that had it not been for the video going viral this would have been another example of over-the-top police brutality swept under the rug and dismissed. Pinnoch's family settled out of court and were awarded monetary damages (Moshtaghian & Sidner, 2014).

In another equally disturbing video from May 20, 2014, an Arizona State University police officer was seen body slamming a young African-American college professor, Ersula Ore, to the ground as she was crossing the street. As was the case with the California Highway Patrol incident, until images of the disturbing incident were splashed over the Internet, little attention was given to the event. In fact, university officials initially sided with the actions of the officer in question believing that "the officer had acted appropriately" until mounting public outrage forced all parties involved to revisit the case.

The officer in this case, Stewart Ferrin, was placed on leave and eventually resigned rather than face termination (Surluga, 2015).

These are just two cases that, due to the determined diligence and conscientiousness of certain individuals who were determined to expose such injustices, eventually received the intense level of attention and outrage they warranted and had initially been deprived of.

Say Her Name

While the names Rekia Boyd, Renisha McBride, Aura Rosser, Kayla Moore, Tanisha Anderson, and Carolyn Sue Boetticher (Sandra Bland being a rare exception) may not have garnered the same level of attention as Trayvon Martin, Jordan Davis, Eric Garner, Michael Brown, and Freddie Gray, Black women are not immune to police brutality. What is even more troubling is the fact that many of these murders and other crimes are often ignored or given scant and fleeting attention by a largely indifferent media. With the sole exception of Renisha McBride, whose killer was convicted in her murder, cases involving the killings and murders of Black women have hardly garnered a blip on the media radar.

Mainstream, and segments of alternative and Black media, yes, *Black media,* need to be taken to task for such gross omission of the value and dignity of Black women. Such behavior (regardless of intent) conveys the message that the lives of Black women matter even less than those of their male counterparts. Such a misguided and incorrect notion is dangerous and must be challenged (VH1, 2015).

It is no secret that Black women have been routinely disrespected and mischaracterized by the mainstream media. Images of loudmouthed, unkempt, sassy, eye-rolling, hand-on-hips, finger pointing, frequently confrontational, obese, baby mama drama, "always wanna fight" images of Black females have far too often been the common narrative associated with Black women. Watching less than ten minutes of *The Real House-wives of Atlanta* or VH1's former program *Flavor of Love* (2006–2008) (Viacom, 2015) gives any viewer a vivid depiction of such images. Black women are seen in the media as the ongoing breeders of unhinged, father-less, violence-prone boys who will eventually grow up and evolve into full-grown criminals.

It is this sort of misguided mindset that sends a large section of the White populace into a state of terror. This attitude is probably a major reason why so many conservative White people wrongly cheered Toya Graham, a single Black mother from Baltimore, for using physical violence against her son during the social unrest that plagued Baltimore during the spring of 2015. The right-wing media perversely and fiercely saluted Graham, championing her as "a good and responsible mother" (Patton, 2015) and she was given numerous media platforms, from both liberals and conservatives, to comment on her behavior. Thus, in the mindset of many on the political right, good Black mothers keep their "thug" sons in line by physically punishing them.

Despite my opposition to her behavior, I can understand why Ms. Graham went "gangsta" on her only son. Many Black people have in fact had a long history of imposing corporal punishment on their children in an effort to keep them in line, coupled with a fear of their children becoming the victim of White violence such as the sort of police brutality that took the life of Baltimore resident Freddie Grey and so many others. The cold hard truth is that Ms. Graham exhibited the very sort of behavior that many of these critics of Black people abhor. More troubling is the fact that the dangerously misguided message Ms. Graham was sending to her son is that he is to accept White supremacy and not challenge it all. By disciplining her son in public and forcing him to leave the protest, the message (in my opinion and others as well) conveyed to her son that he should not challenge unjust behavior by law enforcement, rather he was to accept such blatant injustices.

While many people expressed their outrage at such injustices, there have been those (primarily on conservative-oriented websites) who have resorted to a "they must have done something to deserve it" stance. These are the sort of people who tend to view Black women (and Black people in general) as rude, combative, oversexed, elemental, and not to be trusted. Such a retrograde mentality must be challenged. Black women have just as much right to expect to be treated with a certain degree of civility and dignity by law enforcement as any other group of people. This was why it was so heartening to see the city of McKinney Texas award almost $150,000 to Dajerria Becton, who at the time was a 15-year-old teenage girl who was the victim of excessive physical force by then officer Eric Caseblot. Intense public outcry about the incident led to Caseblot's resignation and eventual dismissal.

This is a necessary and mandatory issue that must be given full attention. Violence of any sort directed toward Black women (or any group of women) is unacceptable.

REFERENCES

Anon. (2015, June 9). Officer caught on video in Texas pool party incident resigns. *Chicago Tribune (Tribune Wire Reports)*. Retrieved from https://www.chicagotribune.com/nation-world/ct-texas-pool-party-video-20150609-story.html

Anon. (2016, September 2). Deputy who tossed a South Carolina student won't be charged. *Associated Press*. Retrieved from https://www.nytimes.com/2016/09/03/afternoonupdate/deputy-who-tossed-a-sc-high-school-student-wont-be-charged.html

Aron, Hillel (2015, December 3). CHP officer who beat homeless woman won't be prosecuted. *LA Weekly*. Retrieved from https://www.laweekly.com/news/chp-officer-who-beat-homeless-woman-wont-be-prosecuted-6345163

Bogado, Aura (2014, August 11). Grandmother assaulted by CHiP officer breaks silence. *Colorlines*. Retrieved from https://www.colorlines.com/articles/grandmother-assaulted-chp-officer-breaks-silence

Carlos P. Sanchez (Director). (2011). *The Real Housewives of Atlanta, Season Two* [DVD]. Lionsgate Home Entertainment. Vancouver, British Columbia.

Hassan, Carmen, & Yan, Holly (2016, September 15). Sandra Bland's family settles for 1.9m in wrongful death suit. *CNN*. Retrieved from https://edition.cnn.com/2016/09/15/us/sandra-bland-wrongful-death-settlement/index.html

Hauser, Christine (2017, June 5). Texas teenager sues officer who threw her to ground at party. *New York Times*. Retrieved from https://www.nytimes.com/2017/01/05/us/mckinney-pool-party-cop-lawsuit.html

Jarvie, Jenny (2015, October 29). Girl thrown from desk didn't obey because the punishment was unfair, Attorney says. *Los Angeles Times*. Retrieved from https://www.latimes.com/nation/la-na-girl-thrown-punishment-unfair-20151029-story.html

Moshtaghian, Armetis, & Sidner, Sara (2014, September 25). $1.5 million settlement for woman beaten by California patrol officer. *CNN*. Retrieved from https://edition.cnn.com/2014/09/25/justice/california-police-videotape-beating/index.html

Nathan, Debbie (2016, April 21). What happened to Sandra Bland? Retrieved from https://www.thenation.com/article/what-happened-to-sandra-bland/

Patton, Stacy (2015, April). Why is America celebrating the beating of a black child? *Washington Post*. Retrieved from https://www.washingtonpost.com/posteverything/wp2015-ou-29

Robins, Norm (2015, May). Three cheers for Toya Graham. *The American Philosopher*. Retrieved from http://www.theamericanphilosopher.com/2015/05/07/three_cheers_for_toya_graham.

Stern, Ray (2015, January 13). Ersula Ore sues ASU for 2 million but ASU supports her move to fire cop. *Phoenix New Times*. Retrieved from https://www.phoenixnewtimes.com/news/ersula-ore-sues-asu-for-2-million-but-asu-supports-her-with-move-to-fire-cop-6635482

Surluga, Susan (2015, February 17). Arizona state police officer resigns after tackling a professor to the ground. *The Washington Post*. Retrieved from https://www.washingtonpost.com/news/grade-point/wp/2015/02/17/arizona-state-police-officer-resigns-after-tackling-a-professor-to-the-ground-for-jaywalking/?utm_term=.f2e456f08bec

VH1 Flavor of Love. (2015). United States: Viacom International, Inc. Retrieved from http://www.vh1.com/shows/flavor_of_love/video

25

Emmett Till: Will Justice Ever Be Served?

The death of Emmett Till resurfaced back into the public sphere in January 2017 with the bombshell revelation that the woman who was at the center of the horrendous saga, Carolyn Bryant, admitted to fabricating much of her account of what happened. A new book titled *The Blood of Emmett Till*, written by Timothy Tyson, a senior research scholar and historian at Duke University (Tyson, 2017), quoted Bryant as saying, "Nothing that boy did could ever justify what happened to him." I think any humane person would agree with this statement.

Till was a 14-year-old boy from Chicago who was visiting relatives in Tallahatchie County, Mississippi, during the summer of 1955. He was kidnapped under cover at night, mercilessly beaten, shot, and thrown into the Tallahatchie River for having the audacity to flirt with a woman. Let's clarify that, he was a teenage Black boy who had the audacity to flirt with a White woman, and a Southern one at that. Bryant asserted that Till whistled toward and grabbed her, while making lewd, crude, and profane comments. She testified to this before an all-White jury during the trial of her husband Roy Bryant and his half-brother J.W. Milam. Till's death prompted a number of demonstrations throughout the nation (Latrice, Fisching-Varner, & Pulley, 2017).

In a compelling article for *Vanity Fair* magazine in January 2017, journalist Sheila Weller passionately highlighted the grim, repressive, restrictive, and terrorizing reality for Black people in the South during this largely oppressive era (Weller, 2017). Anyone with any knowledge of American history knew that an all-White, all-male Southern jury in mid-twentieth-century Mississippi had absolutely no intention of convicting two White men for the murder of a young teenage Black boy, despite overwhelming evidence of their guilt. In fact, in closing arguments, the defense made the case that, as White, Anglo-Saxon men, they had a "conscientious" duty to render a not-guilty verdict.

Several months later, after their acquittal in January 1956, Bryant and Milam gave an interview to *LOOK* magazine in which they were paid for their story and admitted their guilt (Huie, 1956). Milam passed away in 1981 and Bryant died in 1994. Today, Carolyn Bryant is in her mid-eighties and her family has kept her whereabouts secret. Though it happened more than half a century ago, Till's murder was a prime example of how Black men have long been targets of pathological paranoia, hatred, and malice from many segments of society. Black men have been viewed as particularly dangerous to the safety of White women. More than a few bodies of Black men (often innocent) were strung up and hung from trees, burned alive, genitals chopped off, and sold as souvenirs to mentally unhinged spectators who took sadistic delight in such horrid spectacles. Often times, it was due to the words of a White woman. Whether her words were true or false was irrelevant.

The bottom line was that the words of a White woman (or man) took precedence over the words, rights, and dignity of a Black person. As a result, numerous, likely thousands of, Black people lost their lives due to accusations that many people, both White and Black, knew were often untrue (Glanton, 2017).

From the era of slavery to the present day, Black men have always borne the brunt of hostility from the larger White culture. Black men have often been under an unrelenting public microscope, accused of being hypersexualized, perverted freaks of nature. The image of the street thug, crotch-grabbing, Black brute has for far too long dominated the media landscape. These are the sorts of images that have firmly etched themselves in the minds of the larger public and all too often result in negative responses from individuals from all walks of life that Black men are violent, rapacious, menaces to the larger society, and need to be put under control by any means necessary. Till was seen as no different.

The fact that even Emmett Till, a teenage boy, could be viewed as a dangerous threat to the sanctity of White womanhood and White culture in such a reactionary manner vividly demonstrates the lack of humanity afforded to many Black people, then and now.

Despite the fact that she is an octogenarian, Carolyn Bryant and anyone else who is still alive and had contributed to this horrid event should face some sort of justice for their role in the murder of Emmett Till. His more than half-a-century, decades-old blood is on her hands and possibly those of others (Mitchell, 2017). There is no doubt that a number of historical articles, books, archives, and websites will have to be updated to accurately disprove the lies and reflect what actually occurred in this most dark and sordid chapter of American history. The question to ask is: will justice ever be served?

REFERENCES

Glanton, Dahleen (2017, January 30). America always knew woman's Emmett Till story was a lie. *Chicago Tribune*. Retrieved from https://www.chicagotribune.com/columns/dahleen-glanton/ct-emmett-till-lie-glanton-20170130-column.html

Huie, William B. (1956, January 24). The shocking story of approved killing in Mississippi. *Look Magazine*, 46–50.

Latrice, Lori, Fisching-Varner, Kenneth, & Pulley, Tifenie W. (2017). Death by residential segregation and the post-racial myth. In S. E. Weissinger, D. A. Mack, & E. Watson (Eds.), *Violence against black bodies: An intersectional analysis of how black lives continue to matter* (pp. 90–107). New York, NY: Routledge Press.

Mitchell, Jerry (2017, February 6). Could lies about Emmett Till lead to prosecution? *Clarion Ledger*. Retrieved from https://eu.clarionledger.com/story/news/local/journeytojustice/2017/02/06/could-lies-about-emmett-till-be-prosecuted/97557668/

Tyson, Timothy B. (2017). *The blood of Emmett Till*. New York, NY: Simon & Schuster.

Weller, Sheila (2017, January 26). How author Timothy Tyson found the woman at the center of the Emmett Till case. *Vanity Fair*. Retrieved from https://www.vanityfair.com/news/2017/01/how-author-timothy-tyson-found-the-woman-at-the-center-of-the-emmett-till-case

26

Stephon Clark, Antwon Rose, Alton Sterling, Philando Castille: The Devaluation of Black Bodies

The death of Black people at the hands of law enforcement has become so commonplace and routine that many of us who are African-American have managed to become simultaneously outraged and psychologically numb. Over the past few years, we have become front row spectators to grainy and, in some cases, graphic footage of police officers engaged in horrific levels of violent behavior toward people of African descent.

On June 19, 2018, an unarmed 17-year-old teenager, Antwon Rose, a resident of Pittsburgh, Pennsylvania was shot several times in the back as he was running from police. His funeral was a few days later (Bacon, 2018). His senseless and violent death prompted hundreds of thousands of city residents to take to the streets in several days of massive protests (Martinez, 2018) and resulted in the eventual arrest of Officer Michael Rosfeld on June 27, 2018 (Haag, 2018). Stephon Clark, a 22-year-old Black man from Sacramento, California was shot 20 times by police officers in his grandmother's back yard after a brief chase (Del Real, 2018). When officers finally approached his dead body, they discovered that an item that was in his hand turned out to be a cellphone.

As was the case in previous deadly encounters involving Black people and law enforcement, feelings and emotions erupted throughout various communities of all races. Sides were taken and battle lines were drawn. The police union defended their guys. The majority of progressive communities, Black, White, Latino, and others, aggressively denounced what they saw as the violent and callous actions of law enforcement.

The family of Stephon Clark was passionate in voicing their outrage about the loss of their loved one. His older brother Stevante Clark minced no words when he bluntly stated "They gunned him down like a dog. They executed him" (Levin, 2018). No compassionate or reasonable person can dispute this fact. Upon learning of this latest killing of an unarmed Black man, I threw up my hands in disgust. The anger festered inside of me as I seethed with an intense passion. I am certain that I was not alone in my rage.

Stephon Clark and Antwon Rose were just the latest in a series of senseless murders involving young Black men. Two years earlier, in June 2016, the world witnessed another Black man, Alton Sterling, 37, being shot multiple times at the hands of police officers, Blane Salamoni, a four-year veteran of the Baton Rouge Police and Howie Lake II, a three-year employee. In St. Paul, Minnesota, Philando Castille, a father and boyfriend was shot at point blank range by an Asian police officer as he reached for his gun that was licensed. Like Sterling, the 32-year-old Mr. Castile had multiple bullets pumped into his body by St. Paul police. Later that year, in September 2016, Betty Shelby, a member of the Tulsa, Oklahoma police force took the life of Terrence Crutcher, a Black 40-year-old man and Tulsa resident. Each of these men were shot down like animals.

As is routine when such an outrageous tragedy occurs, everyone, in particular the Black community, has been asked to wait for "due process" and to "wait for the facts." Many Black folk braced themselves for the likelihood that justice would fail to materialize, given that this has tended to be the case in similar incidents involving Black citizens. More often than not our assumptions are correct. Blane Salamoni and Howie Lake II, the officers involved in the Alton Shelton case were found not guilty (Bendix, 2017). Jeronimo Yanez was exonerated for the murder of Philando Castile (Smith, 2017). Betty Shelby was acquitted for taking the life of Terrence Crutcher (Juozapavicius, 2017).

As predictable, the standard police defense is that the victim in question was armed, unruly, acting irrational, etc., and thus the officers feared for their lives. In the case of Alton Sterling, the fact that one of the police officers removed an object from his bag drew their (the police officer's) explanation into question. It is important to note that the Justice Department immediately launched an investigation into the matter. Each of the incidents, along with other related incidents, are disturbing on many levels (Wright, 2016). What was notable was that in the case of Philando Castile, Minnesota governor Mark Dayton made it clear that he saw the murder as having racial overtones (Johnson, 2016). During his tenure in the White house, President Obama weighed in on the tragedies that had engulfed our nation, as did 2016 presidential candidates Hillary Clinton and Donald Trump.

Personally, for me, witnessing the 2015 news conference of Quinyetta McMillon, where the oldest child of Mr. Sterling was weeping as he cried out for his father while his mother read an impassioned statement denouncing the slaying of her husband, and seeing his suddenly fatherless children advocating for justice, was indeed a chilling and haunting moment for people across racial lines. Likewise, observing Diamond Reynolds, the then 24-year-old girlfriend of Philando Castile, with tremendous poise, calmly describe the sadistic murder of her lover — how as he lay dying blood poured from his body like a river while her 4-year-old daughter sat in the backseat — was nothing short of surreal. I was immensely impressed. Both situations indicated a clarion call demanding that justice be served.

Predictably, there were certain segments of the media and right-wing trolls who wasted no time going on a perverse form of offense. Some segments of the media brazenly attacked Alton Sterling's character. They made the case that he was a violent man, was a deadbeat father, had a lengthy criminal record, and so on. Personal flaws aside (and we all have our shortcomings), it is probably safe to say that he never fatally pumped four bullets into another human being while that person was pinned on the ground. The entire issue is sickening.

The fact is that, since stepping foot on the shores of America, Black lives and bodies have been routinely scrutinized, objectified, sexualized, and racialized. For many people, Black bodies and Black people, children as well as adults, have never been seen as fully human. All too often, we have been seen as men and women who are largely primitive and invisible, largely denied any degree of humane acknowledgment from mainstream society (Blay, 2016).

One has to ask whether the average White person would be the victim of such random violence by police officers? The answer is absolutely not! The fact is that if White people were routinely and randomly subjected to police violence and were gunned down in the street by law enforcement at the duplicative rate of Black and Hispanic people, there would be calls for congressional demonstrations and cries of protests so loud that it would result in political suicide for any politician or police force who dared to ignore such a rallying cry and decisive message. An equally formidable message must become a reality for people of color as well.

As we all know, there are police officers and other members of law enforcement (arguably most) who are decent, law-abiding human beings who manage to perform admirably doing a job that is undeniably stressful. The horrific murders of five Dallas police officers in July 2016 (six were wounded) — Sr. Cpl Lorne Ahrens, Michael Krol, a nine-year veteran, Michael Smith, retired, Brent Thompson, a recent newlywed, Patrick Zamarippa a five-year veteran — by Michael Xavier Johnson (a 25-year-old army veteran with a disturbing level of racial hatred toward Whites) was another senseless act of violence (Achenbach, Wan, Bermen, & Balangit, 2016). We can only hope their families and loved ones will have embodied the strength to get through such an unspeakable crisis. Honorable police officers aside, the fact is that there is also a faction — one is too many — of law enforcement officials with badges who personify corruption and shamelessly abuse their power.

The problems are numerous and profound: White denial; factions of the right-wing media who routinely suggest the possibility of a race war; the declaration that certain Black organizations such as Black Lives Matter are hate groups; the blaming of Black leaders as racial dividers; and various other forms of intellectually dishonest rhetoric (even certain segments of the left-wing have been irresponsible in this regard). The fact is that Black people are human beings and deserve to be treated with as much respect and dignity as any other group of people. These killings (as well as those of the police officers) are modern day lynchings. Such sadistic behavior and wicked disregard for people of color cannot continue.

REFERENCES

Achenbach, Joel, Wan, William, Bermen, Mark, and Balingit, Moriah (2016, July 8). Five Dallas officers were killed by a lone attacker, authorities say. *The Washington Post*. Retrieved from https://www.washingtonpost.com/news/morning-mix/wp/2016/07/08/like-a-little-war-snipers-shoot-11-police-officers-during-dallas-protest-march-killing-five/?noredirect=on&utm_term=.02927623d0fa

Bacon, John (2018, June 25). Antwon Rose Jr., unarmed teen shot by police officer laid to rest in Pennsylvania. *USA Today*. Retrieved from https://eu.usatoday.com/story/news/nation/2018/06/25/antwon-rose-unarmed-teen-shot-police-laid-rest-pennsylvania/731392002

Bendix, Ana (2017, May 2). No charges for officers in Alton Sterling case. *The Atlantic*. Retrieved from https://www.theatlantic.com/news/archive/2017/05/alton-sterling-case-no-charges/525180/

Bendix, Aria (2017, June 22). Milwaukee police officer found not guilty in death of Sylville Smith. *The Atlantic*. Retrieved from https://www.theatlantic.com/

news/archive/2017/06/milwaukee-police-officer-found-not-guilty-in-death-of-sylville-smith/531222/

Blay, Zeba (2016, July 7). Alton Sterling, Philando Castile and the indignity of black death. *Huffington Post*. Retrieved from https://www.huffingtonpost.co.uk/entry/alton-sterling-philando-castile-and-the-indignity-of-black-death_us_577e6270e4b0c590f7e8265a

Del Real, Jose (2018, March 20). 20 shots in Sacramento: Stephon Clark reignites a furor. *New York Times*. Retrieved from https://www.nytimes.com/2018/03/28/us/sacramento-stephon-clark.html

Haag, Matthew (2018, June 27). Officer who shot Antwon Rose is charged with criminal homicide. *New York Times*. Retrieved from https://www.nytimes.com/2018/06/27/us/antwon-rose-shooting-michael-rosfeld.html

Johnson, Alex (2016, July 7). "Appalled": Minnesota governor says Philando Castile would be alive if he were white. *NBC News*. Retrieved from https://www.nbcnews.com/news/us-news/appalled-minnesota-governor-says-phi-lando-castile-would-be-alive-if-n605496

Juozapavicius, Justin (2017, May 17). Jury finds white Oklahoma cop not guilty in shooting of unarmed Black man. *Chicago Tribune*. Retrieved from https://www.chicagotribune.com/nation-world/ct-oklahoma-police-shoot-ing-verdict-20170517-story.html

Levin, Sam (2018, March 27). They executed him: Police killing of Stephon Clark leaves family shattered. *The Guardian..* Retrieved from https://www.theguardian.com/us-news/2018/mar/27/stephon-clark-police-shooting-broth-er-interview-sacramento

Martinez, Gina (2018, June 26). Marchers block traffic in Pittsburgh as they protest police shooting of unarmed black teen Antwon Rose. *TIME*. Retrieved from http://time.com/5322619/antwon-rose-pittsburgh-protest/

Smith, Mitch (2017, June 16). Minnesota officer acquitted in killing of Philando Castile. *New York Times*. Retrieved from https://www.nytimes.com/2017/06/16/us/police-shooting-trial-philando-castile.html

Wright, Kai (2016, July 7). Why Alton Sterling and Philando Castile are dead. *The Nation*. Retrieved from https://www.thenation.com/article/why-alton-sterling-and-philando-castile-are-dead/

27

John Lewis: An American Icon

I guess no one familiar with the shenanigans of Donald Trump should be too surprised about his ongoing social media habit of attacking anyone who he feels has slighted him. A few weeks before his inauguration in January 2017, the then president-elect took to his Twitter account to criticize US Rep. John Lewis, D-Ga., who made the argument that he saw Trump's election as "illegitimate" for several reasons. In response, Trump brashly referred to Lewis as a person who was all "talk, talk, talk and no action. Sad!" Trump further chastised Lewis for "doing very little" to rectify the problems that afflicted his constituencies. For the record, Lewis represents Buckhead, one of Atlanta's more prosperous districts. As to be expected, criticism toward Trump was bipartisan (Greenwood, 2017).

The fact that Trump would have the unmitigated gall to allude to John Lewis as being incompetent, ineffective, and useless to his constituency is beyond insulting (Smith, 2017). Lewis put his physical and mental well-being in jeopardy multiple times. Who among us can forget the indelible memories of the horrific violence that was unleashed on Lewis — who sustained a fractured skull — and his fellow protesters by Alabama state troopers as they attempted to exercise their right to march for the right to vote?

The sadistic scene eventually became known as "Bloody Sunday," March 7, 1965. Later that evening, several television networks interrupted their regularly scheduled programming to inform the public of the chilling carnage that had occurred earlier that day in Selma, Alabama. Interestingly, "The ABC Sunday Night Movie" that week was *Judgment at Nuremberg*. Talk about irony!

Public outrage was immediate. Educational foundations, religious organizations, politicians, and private citizens from all walks of life flooded the White House with letters and telegrams to urge and, in some cases, demand that Congress move to ensure that American Negroes (that was the term used in 1965) would not be disenfranchised (Pratt, 2016). Something that should have been a basic right from the outset. Intense public pressure culminated in Congress passing the Voting Rights Act (1965) that was signed into law by President Lyndon Johnson on August 6, 1965 (Branch, 2007).

The fact is that, if it were not for people like John Lewis, it would have taken much longer for Blacks, particularly in the South, to gain those protections of the right to vote. Thus, millions of American Negroes would have continued to live under a system of detestable, political apartheid. Rep. Lewis, and many others who marched with him, embodied an undeniable and unmistakable level of courage, determination, and dignity that made it possible for future generations to enjoy specific liberties that some of us take for granted.

The majority of Black people alive today, including myself, were not even born when Lewis, Dr. Martin Luther King Jr., Coretta Scott King, Ralph Abernathy, Juanita Abernathy, C. Delores Tucker, Hosea Williams, C. T. Vivian, Amelia Boynton Robinson, and many others were singing, praying, marching, strategizing, sacrificing, and putting their lives and livelihoods in jeopardy to ensure that so many others who were politically, socially, and economically disenfranchised could exercise a fundamental right that was supposed to be guaranteed to them by the Constitution of the United States.

For Donald Trump to refer to John Lewis and, by extension, others like him who endured horrific levels of wanton violence, routine death threats, cattle prods, foreclosure of property, poll taxes, oppressive sharecropping systems, entrenched legal discrimination, and numerous forms of inhuman indignities on a regular basis as "all talk and no action" is callous and despicable. Moreover, such accusations are blatantly false.

It is a major insult to Lewis and others who forfeited so much without sacrificing their pride and principles. This is in stark contrast to a man like Trump who has engaged in discriminatory practices and made racist, sexist, and xenophobic comments. Trump should be honored that Rep. Lewis would even look in his direction. John Lewis is a living legend who history will undoubtedly reflect favorably upon.

REFERENCES

Branch, Taylor (2007). *At Canaan's edge: America in the King years, 1965–68.* New York, NY: Simon & Schuster. 249–274.

Greenwood, Max (2017, January 14). Lawmakers condemn Trump for attack on John Lewis. *The Hill.* Retrieved from https://thehill.com/homenews/administration/314336-lawmakers-blast-trump-for-attack-on-john-lewis

Pratt, Robert A. (2016). *Selma's Bloody Sunday: Protest, voting rights and the struggle for racial equality (witness to history).* Baltimore, MD: Johns Hopkins University Press. 5–8.

Smith, David (2017, January 14). Donald Trump starts MLK weekend by attacking civil rights hero John Lewis. *The Guardian.* Retrieved from https://www.theguardian.com/us-news/2017/jan/14/donald-trump-john-lewis-mlk-day-civil-rights

Voting Rights Act of 1965, 391 U.S. (1965).

28

People of Color: Continually Demeaned, Devalued, and Dehumanized

When the video of two Black men in Philadelphia being arrested at a Starbucks in April 2018 was exposed for the entire nation to witness, very few Black people were surprised. In fact, when another Black man and his friend were denied permission to use the LA Fitness gym that they both were paying members of, very few Black people were surprised (Jones, 2018).

When Michael Brown, a Black Houston, Texas teenager with a very impressive academic record, earned acceptance and full scholarships to 20 schools (including four Ivy League schools) and was criticized by some FOX news affiliate anchors, many Black people were annoyed but very few were surprised (Shapiro, 2018).

When 14-year-old Brendan Walker sought directions to school and was accused of being a criminal by a White woman and shot at by her husband, many Black people were undoubtedly outraged but not all that surprised (Fortin, 2018).

When a drugged-up, nearly nude, deranged White gunman Travis Reinking opened fire at a Waffle House in Nashville and murdered four young people of color, many Black people (like many others) were undoubtedly shocked, but not entirely surprised (Nielsen, 2018).

Other examples:

- A White graduate student, Sarah Braasch, calls the police on fellow Black graduate student, Lolade Siyonbola, for napping in a room in the dormitory at Yale University that she lives in (Eaton-Robb, 2018).
- A young Black woman being aggressively manhandled at an Alabama Waffle House because she asked why she had to pay for utensils (Edwards, 2018).

- A group of White men call the police on a group of Black women at Pennsylvania golf course for golfing too slow (Caron, 2018).
- A White Jewish man, Aaron Schlossberg, goes on a racist rant against customers speaking Spanish in a Manhattan deli (Racco, 2018).
- Two Black teens are racially profiled while shopping for prom clothes at a high-end department store (Singletary, 2018).
- Two Native American teenagers are questioned by campus police for looking suspect after White mother in the group said the young men made her uncomfortable (Politi, 2018).
- A 65-year-old Black grandmother is roughed up and cursed at by a White police officer in suburban Atlanta (Hansen, 2018).
- A White woman in California calls the cops on a Black family who is grilling at a Oakland campsite (Bennett, 2018).
- Excessive force is used on a young Black man who is roughed up at a Waffle House in North Carolina by a big burly police officer for no apparent reason (Rogo, 2018).
- A White woman gets kicked out of a Starbucks in California for disrespecting two Korean students and demanding that they speak English (Perez, 2018).
- A Black Navy vet is brutally attacked and put in a chokehold by a security guard-bouncer during a minor altercation (Martinez, 2018).
- The granddaughter of reggae legend Bob Marley, Donisha Prendergast, and friends are surrounded and interrogated by police at a California airnub (Hajela, 2018).
- A South Carolina man attempted to hire a White supremacist to kill his Black neighbor and burn a cross in the neighbor's yard (D'Onofrio, 2018).
- A White man approaches a Black woman, a software engineer by profession, and her young daughter, who are vacationing at a hotel pool in Pasadena, California, and asks them whether they showered before entering the pool (Rosenberg, 2018).
- A White female CEO Alison Ettel dubbed "Permit Patty" due to her aggressive behavior, called the police on an 8-year-old Black girl for selling water. Public outrage is intense and she resigns from her job as CEO of Treatwell Health after several clients sever business ties with her company (Chokshi, 2018).
- A White family calls the police on a 12-year-old Black boy, in a Cleveland, Ohio suburb of Maple Height for mowing the lawn. Backlash ensues against the caller and the young man in question, Reginald Fields,

is showered with requests from individuals and businesses throughout the city requesting his services (Williams, 2018).

- In an upscale Atlanta suburb, a White man blocks the entrance of his Black neighbor's driveway (the Black neighbor is a medical doctor) and contacts the police because he refuses to believe that she lives at the residence in question (Boggioni, 2018).

The list goes on.

Driving while Black. Walking while Black. Running while Black. Sitting in a public space while Black. Hanging out by the pool while Black. Asking for help while Black. Eating while Black, Sleeping while Black. Grilling while Black. Campaigning while Black. Merely existing while Black.

To be Black in America is to frequently endure an ongoing state of assaults and insults. Over the past few years, we have witnessed very public examples of Black people being arrested for nothing. Denied access to a health club where they were paying members. Being attacked and ridiculed for achieving academic excellence. Almost being killed simply for being lost and asking directions. Indeed, it seems that being Black is synonymous with being under unrelenting emotional and psychological siege.

It is doubtful — in fact, highly unlikely — that any White man or woman would have been arrested for sitting in a Starbucks without ordering any food or drinks. The fact that they were arrested for "defiant trespassing" (yes, that was the charge) was even more outrageous. It is immensely improbable that very few, if any, White men or women who were regular or even sporadic paying attendees of a health club would be denied, dismissed, and disrespected by management.

With the possibility of some mentally wayward anchors at FOX News and a few other right-wing radio hosts, it is highly improbable that a young White student would be referred to as "ridiculous," "obnoxious," and "showing off." Moreover, we can state with near-universal certainty that a young White teenager would not almost lose their life simply for knocking on a door and asking for directions.

While this is hardly news for those of us who are of African descent, the fact is that such a reality does not resonate for others who are not Black, in particular, White Americans. Consequently, many White people tend to resort to a position of denial. To these Whites, it is not other people, but rather, it is Black people themselves who are the culprits. The usual narratives are: "There must be more to the story." "They must have been guilty." "What were they doing in the neighborhood?" "If they just cooperated with the police." And so on.

Well, the fact is that more often than not, there is nothing more to the story except that another insult or injustice has been perpetrated on the person in question. In her wonderful and deftly precise CNN article, "Why I tweeted the Starbucks arrest video" (DePino, 2018), Philadelphia resident Melissa DePino, the woman who recorded the Starbucks incident on her cell phone, made it clear in no ambiguous language that something this extreme would never have happened to her.

Michael Cohen, a columnist for the *Boston Globe,* wrote a similarly fantastic article about the incident titled "Racism and White privilege in America" (Cohen, 2018). He made it clear that as a White Jewish man, he has sat in more than a few coffeehouses, including Starbucks, utilizing free Wi-Fi, relaxing in comfortable chairs, enjoying the music, sometimes foregoing the option to purchase anything to eat or drink, etc., without ever being scrutinized about whether he had purchased anything. Cohen referred to this as a prime example of White privilege. He is correct.

White denial has long historical roots. The inability of White people to hear Black reality. In some cases, it is the outright refusal to acknowledge such racial, economic, and other related disparities. We have seen such denial manifest itself in the often-hostile commentary that graces the comment sections, Twitter feeds, and Facebook pages of many Whites who refuse to accept the fact that maybe, just maybe, they are in the dark about the many stark realities that face a disproportionate segment of the Black populace in our nation.

Imagine the potential progress for us as a nation if a segment of Whites were able to move away from an unyielding, defensive posture and began to come to the realization that many Black people are not "crying foul" simply for the sake of doing so. That such situations and incidents are far too routine. That the law has routinely been used as a weapon against Black bodies. And that the pain, anger, and despair of Black life is often far too real, and is a message that needs to be heard and listened to with a degree of sincerity and respect that includes not dismissing these individuals as people who are wantonly problematic, mentally disturbed, or irrelevant.

REFERENCES

Bennett, Jessica (2018, May 11). White woman calls cops on black BBQ for using charcoal grill. *Ebony.* Retrieved from https://www.ebony.com/news/white-woman-calls-cops-on-black-bbq/

Boggioni, Tom (2018, June 21). Racist blocks doctor from entering her gated community, then calls cops on her. Retrieved from https://www.rawstory.com/2018/06/watch-racist-blocks-black-doctor-entering-gated-community-calls-cops/

Caron, Christine (2018, April 25). 5 Black women were told to golf faster then the club called the police. *New York Times*. Retrieved from https://www.nytimes.com/2018/04/25/us/black-women-golfers-york.html

Chokshi, Niraj (2018, June 25). White woman nicknamed "Permit Patty" regrets confirmation over black girl selling water. *New York Times*. Retrieved from https://www.nytimes.com/2018/06/25/us/permit-patty-black-girl-water.html

Cohen, Michael (2018, April 20). Racism and white privilege in America. *Boston Globe*. Retrieved from https://www.bostonglobe.com/opinion/2018/04/20/racism-and-white-privilege-america/RHZVq3LTqxCPWd95r5qTUN/story.html

DePino, Melissa (2018, April 16). Why I tweeted the Starbucks arrest video. *CNN*. Retrieved from https://edition.cnn.com/2018/04/16/opinions/philadel-phia-starbucks-why-i-tweeted-the-video-depino-opnion/index.html

D'Onofrio, Kathy (2018, May 10). Man hires white supremacist to hang his black neighbor. *DiversityInc*. Retrieved from https://www.diversityinc.com/news/man-hires-white-supremacist-to-hang-his-black-neighbor

Edwards, Breeana (2018, April 23). Black woman dragged to the ground arrested by officers in Alabama Waffle House over dispute about plastic utensils. *The Root*. Retrieved from https://www.theroot.com/black-woman-dragged-to-the-ground-arrested-by-officers-1825464717

Fortin, Jacey (2018, April 14). Black teen asks for directions: Man responded with gunfire. *New York Times*. Retreived from https://www.nytimes.com/2018/04/14/us/michigan-teen-shot-directions.html

Hajela, Deepti (2018, May 10). Bob Marley's daughter wants accounta-bility for police stop. *Associated Press*. Retrieved from https://apnews.com/1f639b6a11104fc6a03030f04125175a#39;s-granddaughter-wants-accountability-for-police-stop

Hanson, Zachary (2018, May 11). Alpharetta officer resigns after traffic stop with grandmother. *Atlanta Journal-Constitution*. Retrieved from https://www.ajc.com/news/breaking-news/video-alpharetta-officer-suspended-after-traffic-stop-with-grandmother/lPrIdVCNoheNZ4KU8dP6HN/

Horton, Alex, & McMillan, Keith (2018, July 8). #IDAdam, the white male who called police on a woman at their neighborhood pool loses his job. *The Washington Post*. Retrieved from https://www.washingtonpost.com/news/post-nation/wp/2018/07/06/idadam-the-white-man-who-called-police-on-a-woman-at-their-neighborhood-pool-loses-his-job/?noredirect=on&utm_term=.8481d7b8aa87

Jones, Charisse (2018, April 19). LA Fitness says employees accused of harassing two black men no longer with company. *USA Today*. Retrieved from https://eu.usatoday.com/story/money/2018/04/19/l-fitness-fires-threet-wo-black-men-accuse-local-la-fitness-racial-profiling-three-employees-report/531865002/

Martinez, Matthew (2018, May 9). Navy veteran says Texas security guards beat him, stripped him, called him N-word. *Miami Herald*. Retrieved from https://www.miamiherald.com/news/nation-world/national/article210784629.html

Nielson, Kevin (2018, April 22). Half naked man kills 4 people in shooting at Tennessee Waffle House in Tennessee. *New York Times*. Retrieved from https://globalnews.ca/news/4159939/waffle-house-shooting/

Perez, Maria (2018, December 16). Racist woman kicked out of Starbucks for telling Korean students "This Is America Speak English Only." *Newsweek*. Retrieved from https://www.newsweek.com/racist-woman-kicked-out-star-bucks-telling-korean-students-america-speak-750435

Politi, Daniel (2018, May 6). Mom on college tour calls police on two Native American teens. They made her nervous. *Slate*. Retrieved from https://slate.com/news-and-politics/2018/05/mom-on-college-tour-calls-police-on-two-native-american-teens-they-made-her-nervous.html

Racco, Marilisa (2018, May 17). Man's racist rant about people in New York restaurant speaking Spanish goes viral. *Global News*. Retrieved from https://globalnews.ca/news/4214725/white-man-racist-rant-ny-spanish/

Robb, Pat E. (2018, May 13). White Yale student calls police after seeing black student asleep in dorm. *Chicago Tribune*.

Rogo, Paula (2018, May 15). Black man choked by police at Waffle House gives his side of the story. *Essence*. Retrieved from https://www.essence.com/news/black-man-choked-police-waffle-house-gay-slur/

Rosenberg, Eli (2018, June 15). A black woman was at the pool on vacation: A white man asked whether she had showered before swimming. *The Washington Post*. Retrieved from https://www.washingtonpost.com/news/post-nation/wp/2018/06/15/a-black-woman-was-at-the-pool-on-vacation-then-a-man-in-sisted-she-shower-before-swimming/?utm_term=.565c342ebd62

Shapiro, Rebecca (2018, April 9). Fox anchor slammed for calling black teen who got into 20 schools obnoxious. *Huffington Post*. Retrieved from https://www.huffingtonpost.co.uk/entry/fox-5-dc-anchors-black-student-20-colleges_us_5acbdf40e4b07a3485e78869

Singletary, Michelle (2018, May 17). Shopping while black: African Americans continue to face retail racism. *The Washington Post*. Retrieved from https://www.washingtonpost.com/news/get-there/wp/2018/05/17/shopping-while-black-african-americans-continue-to-face-retail-racism/?utm_term=.0b65fd2852dd

Williams, David (2018, July 1). Neighbor calls police on 12 year old boy for mowing the wrong lawn. *CNN*. Retrieved from https://edition.cnn.com/2018/07/01/us/police-called-lawn-mowing-boy-trnd/index.html

29

Pepsi Fiasco Demonstrated the Crucial Need for Greater Diversity in Corporate America

Who can forget the infamous, semi-tragic Pepsi Cola ad with Kendall Jenner of April 2017? Rather than try to describe each controversial and arguably insulting detail in the ad, even though a deal of time has elapsed from its original airing, I would encourage you to view the commercial that has now been pulled. I am sure that you can view it on YouTube or in some other media platform. Even now, well over two years after its initial airing, it will likely answer many questions as well as reconfirm the problems with a lack of representation. As to be expected, immediately after the ad ran, social media across the political spectrum exploded with searing criticisms of the commercial.

Late night TV host Jimmy Kimmel added that it was unfathomable to him that executives in the boardroom would allow such an ad to run, given the current climate (Ahem, 2017). Even Lena Dunham, of HBO *Girls* (2012–2017) fame, a person who has routinely and periodically had her own issues and controversies as it relates to racial and other forms of diversity (Mahdawi, 2017), blasted Pepsi for its actions. British celebrity, now avid Donald Trump supporter, Piers Morgan, Questlove, Jeffrey Wright, Judd Apatow, Patton Oswalt, and other celebrities weighed in criticizing the ad for varied reasons (Calderone, 2017). The words "tone deaf" became the rallying cry of the moment (Belbyck, 2017). Indeed, this was an accurate, spot-on description of the ad.

Bernice King, daughter of slain civil rights leader Dr. Martin Luther King Jr., cynically stated on Twitter, "If only Daddy had known the power of Pepsi" (Hide, 2017). Not to be outdone, Black Lives Matter activist, Deray McKeeson weighed in stating "If I carried Pepsi, I guess I would have never gotten arrested" (Dupree, 2017). Whew, enough said! On the political right, some argued that the ad minimized police officers and made light of law enforcement. Many viewers saw the ad as grossly lacking in taste (Fears, 2017). Black Twitter and much of the blogger-sphere was ablaze with cynicism, sarcasm, anger, and outright disgust. Others targeted the ad for carelessly profiting off protest movements (Solon, 2017). The heat was intense and Pepsi was getting it from all sides (Hyde, 2017). One can only wonder what executives from Coca-Cola were thinking.

After two days, Pepsi officials issued a statement (some argued that it was an awkward, weak apology) and announced that it was pulling the ad and apologized to Black, Latino/a, and other marginalized communities as well as to Kendall Jenner (Lovelace, 2017). "We did not intend to make light of a serious issue," the company said. "We are pulling the content and halting any further roll out. We also apologize for putting Kendall Jenner in this position."

Missteps aside, I don't think anyone, including the critics who were indeed justified in their outrage at such a misguided commercial, believed that Pepsi acted with malicious intent. On the contrary, critics likely conceded that the company was sincere in its intentions. However, the fact is that there are times when even good intentions can go astray, particularly when it relates to issues of diversity and cultural appropriation.

Despite their best efforts, Pepsi managed to insult, minimize, patronize, carelessly objectify, marginalize, and, in some cases, dehumanize people of color, Black Lives Matter activists, victims of violence, and others with a commercial that was far too simplistic and dismissive of the pain and real work that many unsung heroes and others from varied communities are actively engaged in. In essence, the ad whitewashed the often challenging and grim realities facing many people and communities of color. This is another example of White privilege, being able to trivialize and distort the harsh realities that many non-Whites have to endure.

After a couple of days, it became known that there were no Black people in the decision-making process surrounding the decision to make and run the commercial. Upon hearing this, my reaction was "what the hell?!" Now I understood why Pepsi could be so foolish and careless in its actions. This is the real source of the problem. In too many cases where serious and poten-tially consequential decisions are being made, people of color are largely, if not totally, absent from the process (Hobbs, 2017).

Not to say that Black people (or any group of people) are monolithic, but I have to assume that if there had been at least a few Black or non-European Hispanics in the boardroom in question, an entirely different sort of respectable commercial would have aired and Pepsi executives would not have been wiping egg off their perplexed and embarrassed faces. I think many of us who are people of color can concede this point (Jones & Yu, 2017).

Such an unfortunate incident demonstrates the serious need for racial diversity in corporate America and other aspects of society. The fact is that most people know what is acceptable and what is not when it comes to representing their respective communities. Given the rapidly changing demographics of our nation, especially among millennials, and the hundreds of millions of dollars at stake, corporations like Pepsi and others can ill-afford to alienate an ever-growing, racially pluralistic consumer market.

REFERENCES

Ahem, Sarah (2017, April 6). Late night hosts skewer Kendall Jenner's Pepsi Ad. *Variety*. Retrieved from https://variety.com/2017/tv/news/kendall-jenner-pepsi-ad-late-night-hosts-colbert-fallon-kimmel-daily-show-1202024901/

Belbyck, Colby (2017, April 5). Kendall Jenner's new Pepsi ad is so tone deaf, it hurts. *Huffington Post*. Retrieved from https://www.huffingtonpost.co.uk/entry/kendall-jenner-appropriates-the-resistance-to-sell-you-pepsi_us_58e40c27e4b0d0b7e165bdec

Calderone, Ana (2017, April 5). Lena Dunham, Adam Scott and more stars skewer Kendall Jenner's Pepsi protest ad. *People*. Retrieved from https://people.com/food/kendall-jenner-pepsi-protest-ad-stars-reactions/

Dupere, Katie (2017, April 5). Actual activists respond to Pepsi's resistance ad — and they're not having it. *Mashable*. Retrieved from https://mashable.com/2017/04/05/pepsi-ad-activists-twitter/?europe=true#aWTOjdOSosqx

Fears, Danika (2017, April 5). Pepsi is yanking its tasteless protest ad. *New York Post*. Retrieved from https://nypost.com/2017/04/05/pepsi-is-yanking-its-controversial-protest-ad/

Hide, Tylissa (2017, April 5). Bernice King responds to Pepsi ad controversy. *Black Matters US*. Retrieved from https://blackmattersus.com/32057-bernice-king-responds-to-pepsi-ad-controversy/

Hobbs, Thomas (2017, April 7). Pepsi's ad failure shows the importance of diversity and market research. *Marketing Week*. Retrieved from https://www.marketingweek.com/2017/04/07/pepsi-scandal-prove-lack-diversity-house-work-flawed/

Hyde, Marina (2017, April 6). Diet woke: How Pepsi's ad backfired for Kendall Jenner. *The Guardian*. Retrieved from https://www.theguardian.com/lifeandstyle/ lostinshowbiz/2017/apr/06/pepsi-race-luther-king-kendall-jenner-lindsay-lohan

Jones, Charise, & Yu, Roger (2017, April 6). How did Pepsi's ad even get off the drawing board. *USA Today*. Retrieved from https://eu.usatoday.com/story/money/2017/04/06/pepsis-ad-diversity/100133470/

Lovece, Frank (2017, April 5). Pepsi apologizes for controversial Kendall Jenner commercial. *Newsday*. Retrieved from https://www.newsday.com/entertainment/celebrities/pepsi-apologizes-for-controversial-kendall-jenner-commercial-1.13365902

Mahdawi, Arwa (2017, November 25). Is Lena Dunham's "hipster racism" just old fashioned prejudice? *The Guardian*. Retrieved from https://www.theguardian.com/world/2017/nov/25/hipster-racism-lena-dunham-prejudice

Solon, Olivia (2017, April 4). Kendall Jenner's Pepsi ad criticized for co-opting protest movements for profit. *The Guardian US*. Retrieved from https://www.theguardian.com/fashion/2017/apr/04/kendall-jenner-pepsi-ad-protest-black-lives-matter

PART IV

Soulful Reflections on Entertainment, Icons, and Celebrity

30

O.J. Simpson: Still Captivating and Polarizing the Nation

On July 20, 2017, inmate 1027820, Orenthal James Simpson (O.J. Simpson), was granted parole by a four-member Nevada parole commissioners corrections board. He was subsequently released from the Lovestock Correctional Center, which is located in rural Nevada, on October 1, 2017 where he was serving time for robbery (Friess, 2008).

For many people following this story, it was not that much of a surprise. After all, the once former Heisman trophy winner, NFL great, and at one time, all around likable (for some lovable) Simpson, was now 70 years old. Slimmer, gray haired, and notably aged. Since his initial incarceration in 2008 he could hardly be considered the same potential danger or menace to society that he was believed to be a decade earlier, or in the mid-1990s. Truth be told, by the mid-1990s, he was indeed a polarizing figure.

Simpson's reaction at being granted parole was one of genuine surprise and relief. He had the support of one of his sisters, Shirley Baker, and his now 50-year-old daughter, Arnelle, who were present at his hearing. His demeanor was typical of his previous behavior. As he gave his statement, he went on the offensive, even going so far as to state, with a straight face, that he has always "lived a conflict-free life." I can only imagine the number of eyebrows that were raised, eyes that were rolling, shade that was thrown, and other varied reactions that took place upon hearing those words spew out of the mouth of Mr. Simpson. My initial reaction was, please! You don't believe that bullshit yourself!

Over the past two decades, the nation has been captivated by the Simpson case. The initial 1994 trial spawned numerous books, television programs, and a network, Court TV. Many law school professors discuss the trial on a routine basis in their courses and the event has become a permanent fixture in the pop culture fabric of our nation. Prominent journalists routinely write cover stories about him (Coates, 2016). In the summer of 2016, ESPN'S *O.J.: Made in America* and FX's Emmy award-winning miniseries *The People vs. O.J. Simpson* demonstrated society's fascination with both Simpson and the Simpson trial. The trial is deeply etched in many people's memories.

It is safe to say that those of us over 35 years old have vivid memories of the trial. The trial was a television spectacle with all the makings of a potential Hollywood movie. Sex and violence, interracial relationships and marriage, infidelity, alcoholism, sexual deviancy, and a whole host of tantalizing, lurid details that titillated and fascinated the public. Stories covering the trial became daily tidbits as all venues of major media from weekly tabloids, to highbrow publications intensely covered the trial. If these facts were not enough, you also had a cast of real-life characters that would have been a fiction writer's dream.

The strong, handsome, sex symbol, former Black hall-of-fame Heisman trophy winner. The former beauty queen, blonde-haired, blue-eyed murdered wife. Her tall, dark, and handsome, murdered body builder friend. The blonde-haired hedonistic beach boy. The Latin housekeeper. The Asian judge. The White/Jewish female prosecutor. The Black male prosecutor who was held in suspicion and disdain by a number of Black people. The Black male defense attorney who was adored by large segments of the Black community (Monroe, 2016). The legendary WASP attorney. The Jewish defense attorney. The Black ex-wife and kids from his first marriage. Biracial kids from his second marriage. The White racist cop. It went on and on. It was theater of the surreal so to speak.

To be fair, prior to his arrest in 1994, Simpson did indeed live a largely quiet, yet charmed life at least in the public sphere. He was seen by many people as a congenial Black man of immense athletic talent who transcended race. He was a frequent guest in many B movies (in particular, the *Naked Gun* comedies) and a Monday Night Football commentator.

Many corporations such as Hertz Rent a Car eagerly sought him to endorse their products and he was only too glad to do so. He was a very effective spokesperson, in that many Americans across racial lines (in particular, White Americans) liked, in fact, loved O.J. Simpson, and that intense admiration was reciprocated by him. When it came to race, Simpson often took nuanced stances that were designed to not offend White sensibilities on the issue.

Despite his efforts to straddle the lines of racial neutrality, Simpson soon became aware that once he was implicated in the murders of his ex-wife Nicole Brown Simpson and her body builder, waiter friend, Ronald Goldman, the once Black Prince Charming image he had worked so stealthily and diligently to cultivate quickly evaporated. His image rapidly transformed from good Black man to brutal Black buck nigger (Strachan, 2016). The fact that Nicole Brown Simpson was blonde-haired, blue-eyed, and a former beauty queen, and that Ronald Goldman was tall, dark, handsome, muscular, and a part-time model intensified the hatred toward Simpson, particularly in racially conscious and certain restrictive social circles (Dunne, 1995). Race did indeed matter! (Anon., 1995).

While racial animosity toward Simpson was primarily directed toward him by Whites, there was a number of Black folk who made their disdain with Simpson well known. In certain Black circles (not all), Simpson was seen as a White folk's negro, soft shoe, sellout, self-hating negro, and referred to in other less than flattering terms. His Blackness, or supposed lack of, was the subject of fierce debate. By the mid-1990s, he was indeed a polarizing figure. O.J. seemed to be in a racial twilight zone.

Without a doubt, O.J. Simpson is a larger-than-life figure. Save for a rumored incident in Las Vegas in November 2017 that was never substantiated (Rhett, 2017), he has managed to maintain a low profile since his second release from prison. Some have argued that Simpson should not be allowed to profit from his release. Others have argued that Simpson has paid his dues and deserves the opportunity to live his life with as much normalcy as possible.

Both sides are passionate in their stances. However, if we are being honest with ourselves, most rational people know that Simpson was incarcerated in 2008 for failing to be convicted in 1995. The judge and jury in the second trial were determined to see Mr. Simpson face justice for what they saw as his failure to do so in his initial 1995 acquittal. Even most legal experts conceded as much, arguing that under normal circumstances, most people would have received three years, likely less, or even probation for the sort of crime that Simpson was involved in Nevada.

Decades later, even in the current climate, just minutes after his parole request was granted, social media did not miss a beat as it weighed in with avid commentary. Both supporters and detractors wasted no time in letting their feelings be known. Comments about the first trial dominated commentary among detractors. Excessive punishment and racial bias were the preferred words of choice for supporters. One thing that was notable was the fact that almost a quarter of a century later, by 2016, the majority of Whites and Blacks were convinced that Simpson was in fact guilty of double homicide (Ross, 2016).

It is very telling that many of Simpson's critics (mostly White) who have taken him to task (and in my opinion, justifiably so) for two gruesome murders seemed to either overlook or ignore the fact that Claus Von Bulow, Robert Blake, and several other White men were exonerated under similar circumstances. In the case of Von Bulow, he went on to appear on the cover of *Vanity Fair* and became a social fixture in New York society circles.

Moreover, if we are being honest, the truth is that if Simpson had been accused of murdering his first wife, a Black woman and another Black person, the searing level of public outrage and craven level of print and electronic media coverage would not have been anywhere near as intense. In fact, I would argue that it might have been a minor cover story in *Jet* or *Ebony* magazine and not much else. Many online Black websites that cover Black news did not exist at the time. Such attitudes demonstrate that Black lives are too often of little, if any, significance to the larger society.

O.J. Simpson is a larger-than-life figure (Jones, 2017). Many people are hoping he will turn the corner, move on with his life, and stay out of the limelight. Others loathe him and are rooting for his demise and destruction. They say with age comes wisdom. Hopefully, for his sake, Simpson has learned from his mistakes, will make wise decisions, and behave accordingly.

REFERENCES

Anon. (1995, October 6). Races disagree on impact of Simpson trial. CNN-Time Magazine Poll. Retrieved from http://edition.cnn.com/US/OJ/daily/9510/10-06/poll_race/oj_poll_txt.html

Coates, Ta-Nehisi (2016, October). What O.J. Simpson means to me? *The Atlantic.* Retrieved from https://www.theatlantic.com/magazine/archive/2016/10/what-o-j-simpson-means-to-me/497570/

Dunne, Dominick (1995, December). O.J. Simpson: Life after murder trial. *Vanity Fair.* Retrieved from https://www.vanityfair.com/magazine/1995/12/dunne199512

Friess, Steve (2008, October 4). O.J. Simpson convicted of robbery and kidnapping. *New York Times.* Retrieved from https://www.nytimes.com/2008/10/04/world/americas/04iht-simpson.1.16687098.html?mtrref=www.google.com&gwh=20C5D4D597A532FDF68942BF6C2A8A10&gwt=pay

Jones, Jalhan (2017, July 20). The significance of O.J. Simpson in 2017. *Huffington Post*. Retrieved from https://www.huffingtonpost.co.uk/entry/what-does-oj-simpson-mean-to-us-in-2017_us_59709216e4b0110cb3cc5738

Miller, Joshua-Rhett (2017, November 9). "Drunk" OJ Simpson kicked out of Las Vegas hotel. *New York Post*. Retrieved from https://nypost.com/2017/11/09/drunk-oj-simpson-kicked-out-of-las-vegas-hotel/

Monroe, Sylvester (2016, June 16). Black America was cheering for Cochran, not O.J.. *The Undefeated*. Retrieved from https://theundefeated.com/features/black-america-was-cheering-for-cochran-not-o-j/

Ross, Janell (2016, March 4). Two decades later, black and white Americans finally agree on O.J. Simpson's guilt. *The Washington Post*. Retrieved from washingtonpost.com. Retrieved from https://www.washingtonpost.com/news/the-fix/wp/2015/09/25/black-and-white-americans-can-now-agree-o-j-was-guilty/?noredirect=on&utm_term=.61168849f6b4

Strachan, Maxwell (2016, June 14). O.J. Simpson didn't want to be associated with Black America: Then he came to symbolize it. *Huffington Post*. Retrieved from https://www.huffingtonpost.co.uk/entry/oj-simpson-race-black_us_575ee2d9e4b0e4fe51431080

31

Muhammad Ali: Bold, Daring, Authentic, Problematic, and Kept It 100 Percent Real

On June 3, 2016, one of the most well-known athletic figures that ever lived departed this earth. Immediately upon his death, the commentary with regard to his life began. Good, bad, complimentary, critical, and extreme are just a few examples of the sentiments that have graced varied segments of the media (Harris, 2016). Boxer and activist Muhammad Ali, known in his early life as Cassius Clay, was one of the most controversial figures in American history. He engendered feelings of delirious admiration among his supporters and frequently vile emotions from his detractors (Gregory, 2016).

Ali was larger than life — bold, proud, confident, and yes, arrogant. The latter trait was evident in some of his many legendary proclamations such as "I am the greatest," "I'm so pretty," and "I'm a bad man." It also was apparent in his brazen taunting and harassment of Sonny Liston, Joe Frazier, and other rivals. He said what he felt and he spoke what he believed to be truth to power, and was not concerned with how other people felt (Sheinin, 2016).

Ali was a man of principle. While it could be argued that some of his principles were debatable (which can be said of anyone), he still, nonetheless, had them. This was evident in his conscientious objection to the Vietnam War (Chengu, 2016), his refusal to serve, and the forfeiting of his heavyweight title for several years. He was a vociferous critic of the racism that permeated his era and stood steadfastly with Dr. Martin Luther King Jr. and Nelson Mandela and other leaders of African descent at a time when forging such an allegiance with such men was politically, socially, and financially risky. His admiration and appeal were universal (Klis, 2016).

While many other prominent individuals of his time period (the same is largely true today), Black, White, Hispanic, etc. stuck their heads in the sand, looked the other way, and otherwise utilized a "see no evil, hear no evil, speak no evil" approach to issues of racial, and other forms of social, injustice, Muhammad Ali, on the contrary, told it like it was — consequences be damned (Zirin, 2016). Because of his brash, blunt, and brutally candid opinions on a plethora of issues, Ali earned the enmity of many people.

Large numbers of Whites across the political spectrum detested him for his candor in regard to poverty, racism, and other injustices. He also earned the ire of certain Blacks. This was particularly true of older pre-1960 civil rights–era Blacks who, like many of their White politically right-of-center conservative cohorts, saw Ali as an arrogant "negro" (the term used to describe Blacks at this time) young man who was too uppity and irresponsible for his own good, as well as potentially jeopardizing progress for other Black folks.

For all his positive attributes, the fact is that, Ali, at times, could indeed be careless in his rhetoric and contradictory as it related to his religious faith (Gig, 2017). Like many men of his era, he was vehemently sexist and engaged in infidelity. His position on interracial marriage was bigoted, draconian, and he did not hesitate to hurl vicious, verbal hand grenades toward others regardless of whether or not such brutal rhetoric was warranted. This was particularly true in regards to his primary boxing rival, Joe Frazier (Jackson, 2011). His sharp tongue and blunt, acerbic wit earned him numerous enemies. It also afforded him many allies.

As he grew older, even as his health deteriorated and Parkinson's disease decimated his body and silenced his voice, Ali still served as a UN Goodwill Ambassador. He visited children suffering from disabilities, encouraging them with his presence and celebrity, and telling them that they, too, could be destined for greatness. The world stood in awe as we witnessed the former heavyweight champion light the torch at the 1996 Summer Olympics in Atlanta. Just his mere presence at the event caused more than a few eyes to fill with tears as millions were overcome with emotion.

His legend was so powerful that even President Donald Trump considered pardoning Ali for refusing to be drafted during the Vietnam War, which prompted reactions from both Ali's attorney Ron Twell who thanked the president for his overture, but made it clear that such a pardon was not necessary (Sullivan, 2018), and Ali's widow, Khalilah Ali, who was married to the heavyweight champ from 1967 to 1976 and was equally direct, similarly making the case that her ex-husband's conviction had been successfully overturned by the Supreme Court and that such a pardon was not needed. Rather, she made the case for Trump to pardon someone who is currently alive (Estrella, 2018). Sagacious advice indeed.

Muhammad Ali was a controversial, charismatic, magnetic figure who managed to set the world on its heels. In some cases his very presence prompted controversy. He was a man who took people out of their comfort zones. He challenged the status quo. He said it as he saw it and he kept it real. He was Black power, Black Lives Matter, and "say it loud, I'm Black and I'm proud" all in one. He was one of a kind and he will never be forgotten. May he rest in peace.

REFERENCES

Chengu, Gariksi (2016, June 10). Muhammad Ali: How the greatest black athlete in history fought against racism and war. *Counterpunch*. Retrieved from https://www.counterpunch.org/2016/06/10/muhammad-ali-how-the-greatest-black-athlete-in-history-fought-against-racism-and-war/

Estrella, Cicero (2018, June 8). Muhammad Ali's estate says thanks but no thanks to President Trump's possible pardon. *Mercury News*. Retrieved from https://www.mercurynews.com/2018/06/08/muhammad-alis-estate-says-thanks-but-no-thanks-to-president-trumps-possible-pardon/

Gig, Jonathan (2017). *Ali: A life*. New York, NY: Houghton Mifflin Harcourt.

Gregory, Sean (2016, June 4). Why Muhammad Ali matters to everyone. *Time Magazine*. Retrieved from http://time.com/3646214/muhammad-ali-dead-obituary/?xid=homepage

Harris, Keith (2016, June 4). Muhammad Ali, boxing legend, dead at 74. *Rolling Stone Magazine*. Retrieved from https://www.rollingstone.com/culture/culture-news/muhammad-ali-boxing-legend-dead-at-74-180474/

Jackson, Derrick Z. (2011, November 9). Blows of disrespect unfairly pelted Frazier. *Boston Globe*. Retrieved from https://www.bostonglobe.com/opinion/2011/11/09/blows-disrespect-unfairly-pelted-frazier/jhJnUY45HKEd-KGLrt7Fy2O/story.html

Klis, Mike (2016, June 4). How Muhammad Ali was the most culturally iconic, transcendent sports figure of all time. *The Denver Post*. Retrieved from https://www.denverpost.com/2016/06/04/how-muhammad-ali-was-the-most-culturally-iconic-transcendent-sports-figure-of-all-time/

Sheinin, Dave (2016, June 4). Beautiful, controversial, transcendent: Muhammad Ali dies at 74. *The Washington Post*. Retrieved from https://www.washingtonpost.com/

sports/boxing-mma-wrestling/beautiful-controversial-transcendent-muhammad-ali-dies-at-74/2016/06/04/7eb10474-29ff-11e6-b989-4e5479715b54_story.html? utm_term=.9f34546746ea

Sullivan, Eileen (2018, June 8). Trump says he's considering a pardon for Muhammad Ali. *New York Times*. Retrieved from https://www.nytimes.com/2018/06/08/us/politics/trump-pardon-muhammad-ali.html

Zirin, Dave (2016, June 4). The hidden history of Muhammad Ali. *Jacobin Magazine*. Retrieved from https://www.jacobinmag.com/2016/06/the-hidden-history-of-muhammad-ali/

32

Bill Cosby: America's Dad Hoodwinked Us

On April 26, 2018, varied emotions emanated from a number of quarters when renowned entertainer, actor, and megastar comedian Bill Cosby was convicted by a Pennsylvania jury (a majority of whose members were male) of three counts of sexual assault (Puente, Sloan, & Deerwester, 2018). The verdict comes after decades of intense rumors, salacious accusations, and eventually criminal charges. The beloved octogenarian will face three to ten years in prison (Durkin, 2018). His legal team wasted no time in announcing their disappointment and vowed to appeal the verdict. After the ruling, Cosby stood up and hurled a profanity-laced attack at district attorney Kevin Steele who had advocated for Cosby's bail to be rescinded.

There is no doubt that this verdict was seen as a sort of sweet, if belated, justice and vindication for dozens of Cosby's accusers who charged him with sexual abuse, rape, and other forms of sexual violation, and critics took away from that exchange support of their view that he had indeed drugged unsuspecting women and raped them (Boren, 2018). Dozens of women have accused Cosby of sexual assault in incidents that stretch back to the 1970s. There is no doubt that the current, aggressive climate against sexual assault (and rightly so) and the dogged commitment of the #MeToo movement and its largely diverse and pluralistic leadership contributed to such an outcome.

When the charges against Cosby began to surface a few years ago, my reaction to the sordid revelations (like those of many other people) was one of revulsion and disgust. My initial response was "say it isn't so Mr. Cosby!" However, if I am being honest with myself, I have to be brutally candid and say that I was not all that surprised.

In fact, given the disturbing level of deflection, denial, and double speak that Cosby and his various legal teams have engaged over the past several years, why should anyone have been? The current Cosby saga is a tragedy of epic proportions. This is a man that so many people of all races and walks of life admired, looked up to and held up as a paragon of virtue. He was a major television star, author of bestselling books (Cosby, 1996), and an internationally beloved figure. Indeed, his image was so regal that the moniker "America's dad" had been bestowed upon him by millions of people across the globe.

Overnight, we were jilted into a sobering reality and forced to confront the indisputable truth that the Heathcliff Huxtable, warm, loving, stern, competent, confident, and mildly flawed father figure that many of us as young adolescents and pre-teens tuned into NBC to watch on Thursday nights decades ago was anything but (Cooper, 2014). On the contrary, what emerged was a man who embodied a Jekyll and Hyde persona. The celebrity public profile was one of warmth, humor, and affability, and the private man's manipulative, deceptive, sinister, and predatory traits were obscured from an unsuspecting and eventually shell-shocked public (Brown, 2015).

As many cultural pundits and commentators, plain Janes, and average Joes have accurately argued, the fact is that Cosby's self-righteous, intellectually dishonest, callous, arrogant, and acerbic victim-blaming comments, toward those who were often on the receiving end of larger social maladies that continue to cripple large segments of society, was perhaps one of the primary reasons for his spectacular downfall. It also contributed to him being the recipient of stinging and deservedly unflattering commentary (Blake, 2015).

In fact, US District judge Eduardo Robreno cited Cosby's public stance of moral sermonizing and chastising others for their failings to live up to certain principles while he himself (Cosby) engaged in activities that were the antithesis of the moral codes he implored. Thus, this was the reason for him (Robreno) granting permission to allow the release of such graphic and compelling testimony (Weinman, 2015). To be blunt and keeping it real, what Judge Robreno was saying was that "you are a damn hypocrite Mr. Cosby!" (Weiss, 2015).

Moreover, as a Black person who was born prior to 1950 (he was born in 1937), the product of a hyper-segregated America, in Philadelphia, under modest economic circumstances, he should have certainly been aware of the devastating impact that poverty, systemic and systematic racism, sophisticated and subtle discrimination, and lack of access to the mainstream can have on those who are victims to such social inequities and inequalities. Economic and structural racism are undeniable factors in the lives of many poor people of color. Bill Cosby should have known this. Instead of acknowledging such brutal facts, he resorted to espousing and promoting a dangerously misguided form of respectability politics that too often places the responsibility for change on those who are being disrespected (Coates, 2008). His retrograde message was the classic example of blaming the victim, and scolding those who are being oppressed for forces that are out of their control (Cobb, 2014). It was apparent that decades of considerable wealth removed him from any semblance of reality.

Since the controversy emerged into the public sphere, there has been fierce debate within the Black community regarding Cosby. There are those who see him as the latest target of a racist society whose ultimate intention is to discredit and destroy high-achieving, powerful Black men while ignoring or exonerating similar transgressions against powerful, influential White men because of his tough love rhetoric (Peyser, 2015). Others see Cosby as an arrogant, manipulative, self-righteous, hypocrite whom karma has belatedly caught up with (Graham, 2018). I find myself in the latter category. White privilege, in particular, White male privilege is real. That being said, we cannot allow ourselves to automatically resort to blaming racism when our leaders and entertainers have deeply betrayed the public trust. This is the case with Cosby.

From the outset of these revelations, to his eventual conviction, there have been a number of public entertainers, comedians, and private citizens, some public and others in private who have joyously reveled in the demise, destruction, and downfall of a comedic and entertainment icon. Not me. *Schadenfreude* is not something I take pleasure in. There is nothing to celebrate here.

There are no words for the amount of grief, heartache, public embarrassment, and humiliation that Cosby has caused his wife, children, friends, victims, and others in his inner circle. Moreover, to all those fans who did not know him personally, yet saw him as akin to their favorite teacher, lovable neighbor, wise uncle, their own biological father, mentor, or other beloved figure, Cosby disappointed them mightily.

We are all mortal beings and none of us is above criticism regardless of who we are. That being said, Cosby's current crisis and downfall is a prime example of why all of us should tread with caution before we become too overly harsh in our judgment of others for what we perceive to be their shortcomings. We are all mortal human beings devoid of total perfection. Perhaps Bill Cosby should have heeded his own advice and behaved accordingly.

REFERENCES

Blake, Meredith (2015, July 8). How Bill Cosby's "Pound Cake" speech back fired on the comedian. *Los Angeles Times*. Retrieved from https://www.latimes.com/entertainment/tv/showtracker/la-et-st-bill-cosby-pound-cake-speech-20150708-story.html

Boren, Michael (2018, April 26). Bill Cosby verdict reaction: Money can't buy you freedom. *Philadelphia Inquirer*. Retrieved from http://www.philly.com/philly/news/bill-cosby-guilty-verdict-reaction-accusers-andrea-constand-20180426.html

Brown, Stacie L. (2015, July 9). 15 times Bill Cosby was a huge hypocrite. *Rolling Stone Magazine*. Retrieved from https://www.rollingstone.com/tv/tv-lists/15-times-bill-cosby-was-a-huge-hypocrite-73640/

Bukspan, Daniel (2015, July 15). How Bill Cosby's fortune and legacy collapsed. *Fortune Magazine*. Retrieved from http://fortune.com/2015/07/15/bill-cosby-fortune-collapse/

Coates, Ta-Nehisi (2008, May). This is how we lost to the white man: The audacity of Bill Cosby's black conservatism. *The Atlantic*. Retrieved from https://www.theatlantic.com/magazine/archive/2008/05/-this-is-how-we-lost-to-the-white-man/306774/

Cobb, Jelani (2014, November 24). What shielded Bill Cosby? *The New Yorker*. Retrieved from https://www.newyorker.com/culture/cultural-comment/shielded-bill-cosby

Cooper, Brittney (2014, October 29). We must abandon Bill Cosby: A broken trust with women, Black America. *Salon*. Retrieved from https://www.salon.com/2014/10/29/we_must_abandon_bill_cosby_a_broken_trust_with_women_black_america/

Cosby, Bill (1996). *Fatherhood*. New York, NY: Dolphin/Doubleday.

Durkin, Erin (2018, September 25). Bill Cosby sentenced to three to 10 years in prison for sexual assault. *The Guardian*. Retrieved from https://www.theguardian.com/world/2018/sep/25/bill-cosby-sentence-sexual-assault-judge

Graham, Renne (2018, March 4). R. Kelly and Bill Cosby are not being lynched. *Boston Globe*. Retrieved from https://www.bostonglobe.com/opinion/2018/05/04/kelly-and-bill-cosby-are-not-being-lynched/mVkPPwOBp53LQwIArnaYOL/story.html

Norman, Tony (2017, May 18). Tony Norman: The comeuppance of Bill Cosby, moral arbiter. *Pittsburgh Post-Gazette*. Retrieved from https://www.post-gazette.com/opinion/tony-norman/2017/05/19/Tony-Norman-Bill-Cosby-sexual-assault-trial/stories/201705190112

Peyser, Andrea (2015, November 9). Bill Cosby is being crucified for being conservative. *New York Post*. Retrieved from https://nypost.com/2015/11/09/perverts-roman-polanski-and-bill-cosby-tangled-in-political-double-standard/

Puente, Maria, Sloan, Gene, & Deerwester, Jayme (2018, April 26). Bill Cosby retrial verdict: Guilty on all 3 counts of aggravated indecent assault. *USA Today*. Retrieved from https://www.usatoday.com/story/life/2018/04/26/bill-cosby-retrial-day-14-deliberations-resume-after-hearing-defense-star-witness/553644002/

Weinman, Jaime (2015, July 7). Was moralizing — not immoral behavior — Bill Cosby's real undoing? *Mccleans*. Retrieved from https://www.macleans.ca/culture/was-moralizing-not-immoral-behaviour-bill-cosbys-real-undoing/

Weiss, Debra C. (2015, July 7). Judge cites Bill Cosby "Pound Cake" speech in decision to unseal court documents. *ABA Journal*. Retrieved from http://www.abajournal.com/news/article/judge_cites_bill_cosbys_pound_cake_speech_in_unsealing_quaaludes_deposition

Whack, Erin Haines (2018, April 27.) Bill Cosby verdict met with conflicting emotions by some blacks. *Chicago Sun Times*. Retrieved from https://chicago.suntimes.com/entertainment/bill-cosby-guilty-verdict-met-with-conflicting-emotions-by-some-blacks/

33

Prince: Bold, Daring, Black, and Unapologetically Controversial

Like millions of people all over the world, I was stunned to hear about the death of Prince on April 21, 2016. The world-renowned entertainer died at his home in Chanhassen, Minnesota. My initial reaction was similar to my response to the deaths of legends Michael Jackson, Whitney Houston, David Bowie, Maurice White, Natalie Cole, Gil Scott-Heron, Lou Reed, and Glenn Frey, and other music legends who preceded him in death around the same time. Another larger-than-life figure taken away from us far too soon! In this case, a major legend who had touch and influenced so many people from all walks of life (Powell, 2016). To paraphrase a line from one of Prince's more popular songs — the doves were indeed crying.

Prince was an artist who personified the word genius. Indeed, Eric Clapton, beloved songwriter and guitar legend, ascribed the highly complimentary term to the late artist in a very emotional and thoughtful tribute on Facebook (Clapton, 2016). He was a renaissance artist who was admired by many people from varied walks of life.

Prince, at one point The Artist Formerly Known as Prince, before reclaiming his name in 1998, was a complex human being on many levels. Like his fellow baby boomer superstar counterpart Michael Jackson (I will admit that I was more of a Michael Jackson fan yet really enjoyed Prince), Prince was an enigma of sorts. Both men were demonstrably talented human beings who at times seemed to be very lonely, socially awkward, and somewhat insecure about the world around them.

Prince was just one of a number of performers of his era who, like Boy George of Culture Club, Annie Lennox of the Eurythmics, Grace Jones, and others, had no apprehension in championing intersectionality

(Johnson, 2016). For Prince and a number of his contemporaries, androgyny was something to embrace, not shun (Blay, 2016). Prince's altruistic attitude was evident in the compassion and generosity he demonstrated toward fellow artists (Pesca, 2016). Indeed, immediately upon his death, more than a few journalists, artists, record executives, and others mentioned the fact that Prince embodied a Santa Claus persona of sorts, in that he bestowed acts of kindness on many people beyond fellow musicians, including strangers, while preferring to remain under the cloak of anonymity (Hajdu, 2016).

Today, a growing number of men, especially millennials, have no trouble embracing gender-bending behavior. Young men such as Jaden Smith, son of actor Will Smith, Odell Beckham, Cam Newton, Russell Westbrook, Adam Lambert, and others have no problem in defying or, in some cases, outright dismissing what has largely been considered "appropriate" male behavior and social norms or sentiments that were often seen as retrograde.

Long before it was hip to do so, Prince daringly and unapologetically pushed the boundaries of sexual fluidity. He wore garish clothes and explicit attire — scarfs, wigs, high heels, eyeliner, mascara, tight pants — as he brazenly twisted, snapped, and turned in front of the camera for all to see. His language, appearance, and disposition all defied standards and norms (Hall, 2016), had many people wondering and, in fact, intensely debating his racial origin, sexuality, religious beliefs, and other facets of his being. He did not fall into the good guy, bad guy, straight, gay, atheist, religious mold. He could not be safely defined and neatly tucked into any one category.

In his early career, he made moves and engaged in antics that many artists of his era (especially Black male artists) would not have dared to. By doing so, he forced his listeners to decide whether talent superseded other more largely arbitrary and subjective qualities. However, in his later years, after becoming a Jehovah's Witness in 2011, he appeared to adopt positions toward sexual pluralism that were less tolerant and more conservative.

Truth be told, there have been few artists that have been as bold and experimental, and as willing to manipulate music in the manner that Prince did, yet also managed to create music that resonated with so many people across the spectrum. Integrating pop, soul, jazz, funk, R&B, and, in some cases, folk music was second nature to him. Along with Michael Jackson, Whitney Houston, and Tina Turner, Prince was among the few Black artists who were given regular rotation on MTV in the early to mid-1980s, which at that time was in its infancy.

This "I did it my way" attitude was demonstrated in his business dealings. Prince waged a contentious battle with his record company and managed to emerge as the victor. Many argue that he led the movement for future artists such as Beyoncé and John Legend to assert more control over their musical careers. It was as if he had an epiphany of sorts as to how the future of the music industry was going to unfold. It was a smart move on his part.

Like many artists, Prince made some missteps. Films *Under the Cherry Moon* (1986) and *Graffiti Bridge* (1990) were less-than-fruitful efforts. Nonetheless, Prince was bold, daring, visionary, and fearless, in a way that few artists past or present have been. The prolific catalog he left behind was demonstrative of this fact (Grow, 2016). Even after his death, he remains a controversial figure (Berman, 2016), and he remains an enigma of sorts. To be sure, as is the case with all celebrities, he had his detractors and was not immune from occasional tabloid speculation. However, in the case of Prince, such public voyeurism did little, if any, harm to his public image; rather, it further added to his already intensely mysterious persona and galvanized his fiercely loyal group of fans (Gonzales, 2016).

While his influence and presence may be more limited among millennials, for large segments of Generation X'ers like me and younger baby boomers, he was one of the most definitive and pioneering voices the world of music has ever produced. Like many of the greats, he left us far too soon. May he rest in peace.

REFERENCES

Berman, Eliza (2016, May 5). Even in death, Prince remains surrounded by mystery. *Time*. Retrieved from http://time.com/4319123/even-in-death-prince-remains-surrounded-by-mystery/

Blay, Zeba (2016, April 22). Prince's revolutionary, complicated relationship with black masculinity. *Huffington Post*. Retrieved from https://www.huffingtonpost.co.uk/entry/princes-revolutionary-complicated-relationship-with-black-masculinity_us_5719094ce4b0d0042da876d6

Clapton, Eric (2016, April 23). Tribute to Prince. Facebook.

Gonzales, Michael (2016, May 13). Why you don't want to come for Prince. *Ebony*. Retrieved from https://www.ebony.com/entertainment/prince-death-rumors/

Grow, Kory (2016, April 21). Prince dead at 57: Iconic singer and musician leaves behind prolific, groundbreaking catalog. *Rolling Stone*. Retrieved from https://www.rollingstone.com/music/music-news/prince-dead-at-57-62331/

Hajdu, David (2016, April 22). Prince: The moment's end. *The Nation*. Retrieved from https://www.thenation.com/article/prince-the-moments-end/

Hall, Terryn (2016, April 23). When I saw Prince, I saw a vital new black masculinity. *The Guardian*. Retrieved from https://www.theguardian.com/comment-isfree/2016/apr/24/prince-vital-new-black-masculinity

Johnson, Jason (2016, April 22). The politics of Prince. *The Root*. Retrieved from https://drjasonjohnson.com/2016/04/22/the-root-the-politics-of-prince/

Pareles, Jon (2016, April 21). Prince, an artist who defied genre, is dead at 57. *New York Times*. Retrieved from https://www.nytimes.com/2016/04/22/arts/music/prince-dead.html

Pesca, Mike (2016, April 22). Purpleness: How Prince defined the sound of the 80's, even when his name wasn't on the records. *Slate*. Retrieved from https://slate.com/news-and-politics/2016/04/chris-molanphy-on-princes-musical-legacy-and-prisoner-rights.html.

Powell, Kevin (2016, April 25). The day our Prince died. *Huffington Post*. Retrieved from https://www.huffingtonpost.com/kevin-powell/the-day-our-prince-died_b_9774050.html

34

Jemele Hill Spoke Truth to Power

In September 2017, Jemele Hill set Twitter and much of the media world on fire. Indeed, the Internet was ablaze when she tweeted "Donald Trump is a white supremacist who has largely surrounded himself with other white supremacists" (Hill, 2017). As one can imagine, such a comment did not go down too well in conservative media and right-wing circles. Tucker Carlson, Sean Hannity, Rush Limbaugh, and the other usual suspects wasted no time laying into the ESPN host for her remarks. There were those who argued that it was inappropriate for Hill to weigh in on political issues on a network dedicated to sports (Ryan, 2017). White fragility was on the warpath against Hill. Left-wing media enlisted their opinions on the controversy also, with numerous pundits analyzing the situation as they saw things (Lopez, 2017). It became a tug of war of the most intense kind (Rosenberg, 2017). Such hypocrisy was eloquently dismantled by late night talk show host Trevor Noah (Wilstein, 2017).

The right wing ire managed to reach the White House where press secretary Sarah Huckabee Sanders argued that such a remark was a "fireable offense" (Gajanan, 2017). Sanders' comments, in turn, led to several individuals and organizations demanding that the House ethics committee investigate Sanders. While acknowledging the fact that such government meddling can have a potentially chilling effect on free speech, the primary question at the center of the controversy remained: Was Hill wrong in her assessment? Let's examine the evidence:

- In the early 1970s, the Justice Department sued the Trump management for discriminating against prospective Black applicants who were seeking housing in their properties. Both Donald Trump and his father, Fred were named as defendants in the lawsuit.

- He took out an ad in the *New York Times* demanding the death penalty for five Black and Hispanic kids who were charged in the notorious Central Park jogger rape case and decades later refuses to acknowledge his arrogant error and apologize to these men who were exonerated years ago (Trump, 1989).
- Reportedly resented Black accountants managing his money due to what he perceived to be their predisposed, genetic laziness.
- Brazenly re-tweeted racist and anti-Semitic insults from Nazi sympathizers.
- Referred to Mexican immigrants as "rapists and murderers."
- Said that a judge was unfit to preside over a case due to his Mexican heritage (Graham, 2016).
- Was a primary supporter of the sinister "birther" movement—along with Orly Taitz—that promoted the claim that Obama was born in Kenya.

And so on. It does not stop here.

The truth is that Donald Trump has clearly aligned himself with politicians who have well-documented cases of racism in their past. Among them is former US Attorney General Jeff Sessions, whose record on racial issues is so controversial that his nomination to a federal district court was rejected after people who worked alongside him testified that Sessions had made racially charged remarks. Sessions allegedly called a Black prosecutor, "boy," made light about his support for the Ku Klux Klan, and targeted the NAACP, accusing the venerable civil rights organization of not being "sufficiently American" in its values.

Speaking of racism, we cannot ignore the fact that Trump rewarded Steve Bannon, who periodically served as editor of the ultra-conservative Breitbart.com website, as his chief strategist. In a *Daily Wire* article, conservative pundit, radio host, and former Breitbart.com columnist, Ben Shapiro argued that under Bannon's tenure as editor, Breitbart unabashedly embraced the alt-right and other White supremacist organizations and outlets, and allowed the site to become a magnet for racists, sexists, xenophobes, White nationalists, and other assorted racist misfits. Shapiro bluntly referred to the commentary site as a "cesspool for white supremacist meme-makers" (Shapiro, 2016). Given all of the aforementioned facts, Hill's argument that Trump has surrounded himself with White supremacists definitely pans out.

As if anyone needed any more confirmation of this, just look at Charlottesville, Virginia in August 2017. During a weekend of violence, Neo-Nazis and other White supremacist groups walked the streets carrying tiki torches, chanting racist, anti-Semitic, and xenophobic rhetoric that culminated in violence and the death of a 32-year-old, Heather D. Heyer, when self-identified White supremacist James Alex Fields, then 20 years old, rammed a car into her and dozens of other counter-protesters. Fields has since received a life plus 419 years prison sentence (Lavoie, 2019). When given the opportunity to denounce such an atrocity, Trump refrained from doing so, but rather, in a brutally confrontational press conference, blamed "many sides" for the tragic melee that occurred. His remarks garnered praise from White nationalists such as David Duke, Richard Spencer, and a number of right-wing media outlets (Reilly, 2017).

A few days later, he went further and referred to some White nationalists as being "very fine people" (Pitts, 2017). Such comments prompted a number of conservatives and several Republicans to distance themselves from the president. There have been stories that Trump biographer Michael D'Antonio, and others who have interviewed the Trump family, in particular, Donald's father Fred Trump Sr., have found that they were strong believers in eugenics and White intellectual superiority. To the question of whether Donald Trump is a White supremacist? To quote the old saying. "If it looks like a duck, talks like a duck, quacks like a duck …"

Rather than take a moral principled stand and support their employee, ESPN quaked in their boots, punked out, and issued apologies to all parties that were offended (primarily conservative right wingers) by Ms. Hill's comments (Roddy, 2017). Indeed, the behavior among the sports network was so weak that it reminded viewers of a desperate spurned lover who was still stalking the man or woman who rejected them. The networks erratic ratings undoubtedly contributed to executives taking such a defensive posture (Holloway, 2017). It appeared money and profits superseded any form of principles including free speech. Damage control was in full force (Deitsch, 2017).

The reaction to Jemele Hill from certain quarters once again highlighted just how entrenched the issue of race still is in the psyche of American society. This was evident from the observation that many Whites are still clearly uncomfortable with non-Whites, in particular Black people, calling out racism or racial injustice. The fact that Hill is female magnified the level of dissention. No doubt, some sexist men resent that she is employed by a network that caters to men's interests. She is also an outspoken feminist of color (Judge, 2017). Thus, being a woman of color, in her case, a Black woman, Jemele Hill was/is caught between the intersection of race and gender (Giddings, 1984).

The more important question is: why was there such vitriol for Jemele Hill as she exercised her first amendment rights whereas Donald Trump, as of yet, has never paid any significant penalties for his blatant White nationalist rhetoric? (Richardson, 2017) Many of us who are people of color already know the answer.

REFERENCES

Anon. (2017, October 10). ESPN suspends anchor Jemele Hill for violating social media rules. *ESPN*. Retrieved from http://www.espn.com/espn/story/_/id/20971317/espn-anchor-jemele-hill-suspended-2-weeks-second-violation-social-media-rules

Arceneaux, Michael (2017, September 14). Why the White House attack on ESPN's Jemele Hill is terrifyingly hypocritical. *Complex*. Retrieved from https://www.complex.com/sports/2017/09/white-house-attack-jemele-hill-hypocritical

Deitsch, Richard (2017, September 13). ESPN employees respond to Jemele Hill controversy over Trump comments. *Sports Illustrated*. Retrieved from https://www.si.com/tech-media/2017/09/13/jemele-hill-espn-colleagues-respond-trump-twitter-comments

Gajanan, Mahita (2017, September 13). An ESPN commentator called Trump a white supremacist: The White House said it is a "Fireable Offence". *Time Magazine*. Retrieved from http://time.com/4940156/espn-jemelle-hill-white-house-donald-trump/

Giddings, Paula (1984). *When and where I enter: The impact of black women on race and sex in America*. New York, NY: William Morrow.

Graham, David (2016, June 2). Trump: Mexican American has an absolute conflict. *The Atlantic*. Retrieved from https://www.theatlantic.com/politics/archive/2016/06/trump-mexican-judge/485429/

Hill, Jemele (2017, September 11). Twitter.

Holloway, Daniel (2017, September 13). Jamele Hill controversy magnified trouble at ESPN. *Variety*. Retrieved from https://variety.com/2017/tv/news/jemele-hill-white-supremacist-trump-espn-1202557572/#!

Judge, Monique (2017, September 27). Jemele Hill and the social burden of being a black woman in media. *The Root*. Retrieved from https://www.theroot.com/jemele-hill-and-the-social-burden-of-being-a-black-woma-1818867174

Lavoie, Denise (2019, July 15). Man sentenced to 2nd life term in Charlottesville attack. *Associated Press*. Retrieved from https://www.dailyherald.com/article/20190715/news/307159989

Lopez, German (2017, October 10). Donald Trump's war with ESPN and Jemele Hill, explained. *Vox*. Retrieved from https://www.vox.com/identities/2017/9/15/16313800/trump-jemele-hill-espn-white-supremacist

Pitts, Leonard (2017, September 15). Since he walks like a racist and talks like a racist. *Miami Herald*. Retrieved from https://www.miamiherald.com/opinion/opn-columns-blogs/leonard-pitts-jr/article173628156.html

Reilly, Kaite (2017, August 15). White supremacists loved President Trump's latest comments on Charlottesville. *Time Magazine*. Retrieved from http://time.com/4902308/white-nationalists-supremacists-donald-trump-charlottesville/

Richardson, Gerald C. (2017, September 20). Jemele Hill told the truth, and the proof is in Trump's own words. *Times Free Press*. Retrieved from https://www.timesfreepress.com/news/opinion/columns/story/2017/sep/20/richardson-jemele-hill-told-truth-and-protrum/449956/

Roddy, Tom (2017, September 13). ESPN apologizes after host Jemele Hill calls Donald Trump a white supremacist. *Newsweek*. Retrieved from https://www.newsweek.com/sport-espn-donald-trump-664744

Rosenberg, Michael (2017, September 14). The reaction to Jemele Hill's choice of words shows how controversy escalates. *Sports Illustrated*. Retrieved from https://www.si.com/tech-media/2017/09/14/jemele-hill-espn-donald-trump-white-supremacist-comments-tweets

Ryan, Shannon (2017, September 18). "Stick to sports" or stick to reality? Jemele Hill controversy highlights media issues. *Chicago Tribune*. Retrieved from *Chicago Tribune*.

Shapiro, Ben (2016, August 24). What is the alt-right? *The Daily Wire*. Retrieved from https://www.dailywire.com/news/8638/what-alt-right-ben-shapiro

Trump, Donald (1989, May 1). Bring back the death penalty! Bring back our police! *New York Daily News*.

Wilstein, Matt (2017, September 15). Daily show nails right-wing hypocrisy on Jemele Hill. *The Daily Beast*. Retrieved from https://www.thedailybeast.com/daily-show-nails-right-wing-hypocrisy-on-jemele-hill

35

Donald Trump and the NFL: The Politics of White Fragility and White Supremacy

On May 23, 2018, NFL owners approved of a national anthem policy that prohibits players from kneeling or protesting during the national anthem (Maske, 2018). Reaction was immediate and the public was largely divided along political lines with many liberals and progressives assailing the ruling and a larger number of conservatives and people on the right lauding the decision. A number of NFL players made clear of their displeasure at the ruling, making the case that they had not been consulted about the matter before it was implemented. There were owners such as New York Jets chairman, Christopher Johnson who vowed to pay the fines for any of his players who made the decision to dissent and kneel during the anthem.

This decision was just another in a number of sordid controversies that have erupted into the public sphere during the Trump presidency. What was seen as an issue that was losing steam in the court of public opinion, after several months of intense debate, was reignited in September 2017 when, at a rally in Alabama, President Trump spoke about NFL players who — during the playing of the national anthem — had been silently protesting social injustice. Trump told the crowd that players who refused to salute the American flag were "disrespectful," "unpatriotic," and should be fired for their actions (Graham, 2017).

Reaction was swift, most notably in the NFL where owners, players, and others condemned what they saw as Trump's irresponsible and divisive comments (Serwer, 2017). Resistance manifested itself in the form of even more coaches and players locking arms, holding hands, kneeling together, and engaging in other various forms of protest. It was civil disobedience at its best.

Given that he has the discipline and temperament of an unruly 5th grader, Trump was unwilling to acknowledge his callous and careless comments. He could have, more sensibly, focused his attention on the crisis in Puerto Rico, the US Virgin Islands, health care, and other immediate concerns that dominated the news at the time. These were/are issues that directly affect the lives of millions of Americans across racial lines. However, being civil, presidential, and a bridge builder is not in Trump's nature. On the contrary, engaging in polarizing and divisive rhetoric is.

He just had to keep the fires burning; that's how he rolls. The president was all too willing to feed tasty red meat peppered with racially tinged venom to the predominately White southern crowd. He knew that this was the type of coded anti-Black, anti-minority, anti-progressive message that more than a few of his reactionary followers crave (Hamilton, 2017). They devoured such rhetoric.

Despite his many shortcomings, Trump is tuned in to the values, sentiment, and mood of his political base. This is a voting bloc that is largely White, extremely conservative, often racist, anti-Semitic, isolationist, homophobic, xenophobic, and fragile like Trump himself (Zirin, 2017). These are the voters for whom the issues of God, guns, and gays (and more recently immigrants and non-Whites) are perennial staples (Rios, 2016). These are the men and women to whom the American flag is sacred. One of valor and honor. A symbol of freedom, faith, and justice.

On the contrary, for many people of color, America is a nation that has not lived up to such principles. These are the people who see their siblings, relatives, communities, and minorities in general routinely denounced, denigrated, disenfranchised, and, in many cases, outright dismissed by a mainstream society that sees them as less than equal or fully human (Bryant, 2018). People whose lives are often rendered meaningless by others.

The nation is witnessing battle lines being drawn in relation to racism, White supremacy, and various other social issues not seen in America since the 1960s. It is somewhat ironic, perhaps even unsettling, given the fact that almost a decade ago, a considerable swath of the nation banded together to elect a Black man to the world's most prestigious office. Americans across racial and socio-economic lines rejoiced at the fact that a nation that had only ratified a Civil Rights bill into law in 1964 (377,1964) and a Voting Rights Act in 1965 (391,1965) was able to elect a man of color to the presidency 44 years later!

To be sure, there were more than a few others who were deeply resentful of what had transpired. Rather, they saw the election of a Black president as an affront to their heritage, values, and history (Blow, 2016). Indeed, throughout the eight years of President Obama's tenure, more than a few of his detractors (mostly White) seethed in anger and resentment. They further unleashed their outrage on right-wing blogs, talk radio, op-ed pages of conservative newspapers, private clubs, secret societies, and for others in selective, often restricted venues (McGirt, 2017). Thus, to this racially disgruntled crowd, Trump's election to the presidency in November 2016 signified a restoration of Eurocentric culture and Whiteness in general.

Moreover, the alt-right and other right-wing Whites became deeply emboldened by his victory and further utilized his presidential victory to promote their radical, yet socially draconian agenda of racial politics. These are the people who embrace a Dred Scott policy as it relates to Blacks and other non-Whites. They have put away the dog whistles and have brought out their racially spewing bullhorns. They have been aided and abetted by President Trump as he has eagerly and shamelessly embraced the actions of White supremacists, referring to some of those individuals as "very fine people." Such behavior from a commander-in-chief is unfathomable in the twenty-first century.

The fact that so many coaches, owners, players, entertainers, businessmen, fans, and citizens in general initially joined together and supported dissenting players, denounced Trump's comments, and avidly defended the First Amendment was inspiring (Lipsyte, 2017). Unfortunately, we saw that in the case of the NFL, economic revenue and fan sentiment outweighed freedom of expression.

While focusing on social injustice is important, indeed imperative, the truth is that there is a danger that too many people will become focused on the NFL, Hollywood, etc., and other more glamorous, sexy issues as opposed to remembering Colin Kaepernick's protest against police brutality and other forms of racial injustice, such as President Trump and the Republican Party frantically doing everything in their power to dismantle the legacy of the Nation's first Black president (Coates, 2017). We cannot allow this crucial message to get lost. The results of the off-year elections of 2017 where numerous progressive candidates were elected to public office were deeply inspiring. For the moment, momentum appears to be moving in the right direction. We can only hope that such progress will continue.

REFERENCES

377 U.S. (1964).
391 U.S. (1965).

Blow, Charles (2016, August 4). Trump reflects white male fragility. *New York Times*. Retrieved from https://www.nytimes.com/2016/08/04/opinion/trump-reflects-white-male-fragility.html

Bryant, Howard (2018). *The heritage: Black athletes, a divided America, and the politics of patriotism*. New York, NY: Beacon Press.

Coates, Ta-Nehisi (2017, October). The first White President: The foundation of Donald Trump's presidency is the negation of Barack Obama's legacy. *The Atlantic*. Retrieved from https://www.theatlantic.com/magazine/archive/2017/10/the-first-white-president-ta-nehisi-coates/537909/

Graham, Bryan A. (2017, September 21). Donald Trump blasts NFL anthem protestors: Get that son of a bitch off the field. *The Guardian*. Retrieved from https://www.theguardian.com/sport/2017/sep/22/donald-trump-nfl-national-anthem-protests

Hamilton, Shawn (2017, October 10). The real reason Donald Trump is targeting NFL owners rather than protesting players. *The Intercept*. Retrieved from https://theintercept.com/2017/10/10/donald-trump-nfl-owners-national-anthem-protests/

Lipsyte, Robert (2017, October 19). Is Donald Trump saving the NFL? *The Nation*. Retrieved from https://www.thenation.com/article/is-donald-trump-saving-the-nfl/

Maske, Mark (2018, May 23). NFL owners approve new national anthem policy with hopes of ending protests. *The Washington Post*. Retrieved from https://www.washingtonpost.com/news/sports/wp/2018/05/23/nfl-owners-leaning-towards-requiring-players-to-stand-for-national-anthem-or-remain-in-locker-room/?utm_term=.34b6d7d4c0d1

McGirt, Ellen (2017, February 17). The president and white fragility. *Fortune*. Retrieved from http://fortune.com/2017/02/17/the-president-and-white-fragility/

Rios, Carmen (2016, November 13). How Donald Trump's election reveals the danger of white male fragility. *Everyday Feminism Magazine*. Retrieved from https://everydayfeminism.com/2016/11/donald-trump-white-male-fragility/

Serwer, Adam (2017, September 23). Trump's war of words with black athletes. *The Atlantic*. Retrieved from https://www.theatlantic.com/politics/archive/2017/09/trump-urges-nfl-owners-to-fire-players-who-protest/540897/

Zirin, Dave (2017, September 24). The fragile toxic masculinity of Donald Trump. *The Nation*. Retrieved from https://www.thenation.com/article/the-fragile-toxic-masculinity-of-donald-trump/

36

Bill Maher, and the Nigger-Word Debate

On June 9th, 2017, Bill Maher, host of the quasi-political/entertainment program HBO *Real Time with Bill Maher*, had renowned Black intellectual and ordained Baptist minister Dr. Michael Eric Dyson and rapper/actor Ice Cube as guests. They discussed the controversy that erupted on the June 2nd edition of the program when Maher flippantly referred to himself as a "house nigger" in an interview with Sen. Ben Sasse (R-Neb). The senator had been invited to the program to discuss his book on what he perceived as the increasing problem on prolonged adolescence occurring in American society. Sasse and Maher agreed on the issue and provided examples and suggestions on how to rectify the problem. Things seemed to be going well up until this exchange transpired between both men:

> Maher: Adults dress up for Halloween. They don't do that in Nebraska?
> Sasse: It's frowned upon. We don't do that quite as much.
> Maher: I gotta get to Nebraska more.
> Sasse: You're welcome. We'd love to have you work in the fields with us.
> Maher: Work in the fields? Senator, I'm a house nigger.
>
> (HBO, June 2, 2017)

Audience reaction was mixed. Some laughed while others simultaneously groaned. Sasse's body language betrayed a visible level of shock and discomfort despite his stiff grin. Maher, quickly commented that "he made a joke" and proceeded on with the conversation. Well, many people were not so ready to move on. Reaction on social media was swift and intense. The Internet was popping with controversy. Not surprisingly much of Black Twitter

168

went to town denouncing Maher for his juvenile antics and more than a few went as far as accusing him of outright racism (Littleton, 2017).

Numerous people, including Black Lives matter activist Deray McKeeson demanded that HBO cancel his program (Durden, 2017). Some felt that the incident was much ado about something relatively minor (Jabbar, 2017). Then there were others, who stated that they understood and realized where Bill Maher was coming from with his comments, yet, gave him a verbal backhanded slap upside the head and a nice, yet candid warning about his occasional verbal recklessness (Morris, 2017).

A few days later, Senator Sasse weighed in on the controversy stating that he should have challenged Maher for making such a comment (Politi, 2017). Others argued that his status as a comedian provided Maher with permission to espouse such language (Cote, 2017). Within 24 hours, Maher issued an awkward apology (St. Felix, 2017). He further stated that his actions were "inexcusable and tasteless" (Pengelly, 2017). It is important to note that both Professor Dyson and Ice Cube confronted Maher and schooled him (Maher) about his actions (Jackson, 2017).

As someone who was watching the program when Maher made his comment, I will admit that I was somewhat blindsided by the comment. That being said, I was not enraged. In fact, I actually responded with a mild chuckle in the way that people usually respond to people who make comments that are inappropriate, yet not so totally over the top. I know that it would be very easy, perhaps even socially appropriate to have taken to social media and express self-righteous anger over the transgressions of a wealthy White man having the audacity to use the N-word in a thoughtless manner. However, it is probably safe to say that many Black folk were not as outraged as they feigned to be about the situation, though a number of Black people undoubtedly were disturbed by such language. Mildly shocked? Yes. Outraged? Probably not.

Yes, I think there were some people deeply engaged in a level of intellectual dishonesty, or what we refer to as fake outrage. To be sure, I have my issues with Bill Maher. His crass sexism, brutish Islamophobia, smug self-righteousness, deep personal insecurities, and annoyingly outright "ain't I a devil. I am obnoxious because I can be" attitude leaves much to be desired. As others have mentioned, his paternalistic sort of liberalism can be deeply offensive (Hazzell, 2017). He can indeed be a jerk at times.

That being said, when it comes to racial issues, while he occasionally misfires, he does frequently get it right. He often delves into areas such as police brutality, systemic and systematic racism, White indifference, etc., which most comedians, in particular White comedians, often do not dare go anywhere near. He does try to keep it as real as possible. To act as if he is some rabid White confederate who gets in a pickup truck, rides around, and screams White Power at the top of his lungs or attends White Citizen Council meetings advocating for policies that systemically and systematically discriminate against Black people is being intellectually dishonest and most of my fellow Black brethren know this (Taylor, 2017). Moreover, who among us is perfect?

Now, let me make it clear, as someone who is Black, a historian by training, and over 50 years old, I am well aware of both the brutal history and the inherent power and pain associated with the word nigger. No word better reflects the oppression that we as people of African descent have faced. From a historical perspective, the word is one that is rooted in violence, humiliation, denigration, degradation, and other forms of inhumane treatment. Indeed, it has been used by a number of White people as a physical and psychological weapon against us. To be sure, some Black folk have taken the word and internalized it as a form of self-scorn and hatred. On the contrary, others have taken the word, neutralized it, and used it as a term of admiration or endearment.

Nonetheless, like a number of historically marginalized groups, Black Americans have managed to take the word and somewhat neutralize and redefine it, just as gay and lesbians have managed to take the words queer and dyke and turn them into a form of empowerment to the LGBTQ community. I also concur with the notion that Whites should not use the word.

To all those who want to cry foul or espouse the misguided notion of double standards and other indefensible sentiments, the truth is that the word nigger has a hostile and obscene history in the White community. It has been employed with violence (as in the lynchings and murders of Black people), malice, blatant disrespect, intimidation, and varied forms of humiliation. From a historical perspective, there is nothing ambiguous about its use. Whereas, in the Black community, even centuries after its origin, the word has a mixed and unsettled history. Thus, ongoing debates in regards to its usage are understandable.

Without sounding too sanctimonious, the fact is that the Black community is being confronted with a number of issues and people who likely view and treat us like "niggers" (although in my case I tend to give as good as I get) whether we use the n-word or not. The winds of racism, White supremacy, and xenophobia are rapidly fermenting both in America and abroad. White identity politics is showing its racially thirsty saber teeth. Charlottesville 2017 anyone? Racial harassment of non-Whites has literally become a daily occurrence.

We currently have an administration that is cutting hundreds of millions of dollars from public education that disproportionately impacts poor and lower-income Black and Hispanic communities, working to enact some of the most draconian social and economic policies not seen in our nation since the 1920s, gutting after-school programs, and working diligently to repeal the Affordable Care Act (it has been gutted considerably since 2017) and replace it with the draconian Trumpcare or some other retrograde plan. The list goes on.

While we need to continue to have healthy and robust debates on the n-word and other topics that affect our community, it is important that we not get too sidetracked from crucial economic, legal, and social issues that directly impact us on a daily basis. Failing to do so could lead to our overall detriment. We must keep our eyes on the prize for survival's sake. Debating and reacting to the n-word on a 24/7 basis is not the best use of our time, energy, and resources. Words for thought.

REFERENCES

Cote, Rachel V. (2017, June 10). Bill Maher says using N-word was a "Bad thing but also a Comedian Thing". Retrieved from https://jezebel.com/bill-maher-says-using-n-word-was-a-bad-thing-but-also-a-1795984866

Durden, Tyler (2017, June 3). Liberals outraged, demand termination after Bill Maher says "I'm a House Ni**er". *Zero Hedge*. Retrieved from https://www.zerohedge.com/news/2017-06-03/liberals-outraged-after-bill-maher-says-im-house-nier

Hazzell, Ricardo A. (2017, June 6). Bill Maher and his poisonous brand of white liberalism. *The Shadow League*. Retrieved from https://theshadowleague.com/the-n-word-why-bill-maher-can-never-go-too-far-with-blacks/

Jabbar, Kareem A. (2017, June 7). No Bill Maher shouldn't be fired for using the N-word. *The Hollywood Reporter*. Retrieved from https://www.hollywoodreporter.com/news/kareem-abdul-jabbar-no-bill-maher-shouldnt-be-fired-using-n-word-1010907

Jackson, Cherese (2017, June 12). Ice cube educates Bill Maher on use of the "N" word. *Liberty Voice*. Retrieved from https://guardianlv.com/2017/06/ice-cube-educates-bill-maher-use-n-word-video/

Littleton, Cynthia (2017, June 30). Bill Maher, HBO face backlash after host uses racial slur on "real time". *Variety*. Retrieved from https://variety.com/2017/tv/news/bill-maher-n-word-backlash-reaction-1202453193/

Maher, Bill (2017). *Real Time with Bill Maher*. HBO Television.

Maher, Bill (2017, June 2). *Real Time with Bill Maher*. HBO Television.

Maher, Bill (2017, June 9). *Real Time with Bill Maher*. HBO Television.

Morris, Wesley (2017, June 4). What was Bill Maher's big mistake? *New York Times*. Retrieved from https://www.nytimes.com/2017/06/04/arts/television/what-was-bill-mahers-big-mistake.html

Pengelly, Martin (2017, June 3). Bill Maher sorry for use of N-word as HBO calls it "inexcusable and tasteless". *The Guardian*. Retrieved from https://www.theguardian.com/tv-and-radio/2017/jun/03/bill-maher-hbo-real-time-ben-sasse

Politi, Daniel (2017, June 3). GOP senator: I should have spoken up when Bill Maher used N-word. *Slate*. Retrieved from https://slate.com/news-and-politics/2017/06/sen-ben-sasse-i-should-have-spoken-up-when-bill-maher-used-n-word-in-interview.html

St. Felix, Doreen (2017, June 12). Bill Maher's weird, effortful apology for saying the N-word. *The New Yorker*. Retrieved from https://www.newyorker.com/culture/culture-desk/bill-mahers-weird-effortful-apology-for-saying-the-n-word

Taylor, Shaun T. (2017, June 5). The "N" word: When to be offended. *Chicago Defender*. Retrieved from https://chicagodefender.com/2017/06/05/the-n-word-when-to-be-offended/

37

Roseanne Barr and the Politics
of Right-Wing Hypocrisy

On June 21, 2018, ABC announced that it was developing a *Roseanne* spinoff entitled "The Conners" (Acuna, 2018). Upon hearing the news, public reaction was mixed. There were those who felt that Barr's co-stars and the hundreds of cast and crew members who worked on the program were unfairly punished due to her (Barr's) callous insensitivity, and thus a reboot minus Roseanne herself was appropriate. Other people felt that the remake should never have been made and that the recent cancellation should remain (Martin, 2018). There is no doubt that executives at ABC spent considerable time weighing the pros and cons of a reboot, with the pros apparently outweighing the cons. To put it more bluntly, money talks!

This series of events came on the heels of several previous weeks of drama for Barr and ABC. On May 29, 2018, the controversial comedian was terminated by ABC and her revised, updated sitcom was canceled (Koblin, 2018). It was only a matter of hours before that the public were witness to the despicable comments she tweeted: "Muslim brotherhood & Planet of the apes had a baby" referring to Valerie Jarrett, the Black former senior adviser to President Barack Obama.

Without surprise, social media reaction was fast, swift, and furious. ABC wasted no time in delivering its decision to terminate Barr. Channing Dungey, president of ABC News Entertainment division, and the first Black woman to hold the position, was swift in her condemnation.

"Roseanne's Twitter statement is abhorrent, repugnant and inconsistent with our values, and we have decided to cancel her show," Dungey said. She was routinely applauded for taking such decisive action and won the support of Robert Iger, the CEO of Disney, as well as other public figures (Dungey, ABC 2018).

It should be noted that this was not the first time Barr has ventured into crude, callous territory as it relates to race. In 2013, she referred to Susan Rice, national security adviser in the Obama administration, as a "man with big swinging ape balls." Roseanne engaged in the most racially primitive language possible. Comparing Black people to apes, monkeys, animals, and other non-human or less-than-human species is classic, primitive racist rhetoric straight out of the pages of regressive, old-fashioned, eugenic-minded, racial stereotypes.

Initially, rather than take responsibility for her own despicable comments, Barr blamed anything and everyone else. Comedian Wanda Sykes who served as a consultant for the program (a fact in and of itself that seems questionable) and promptly quit after Barr posted her retrograde, bigoted comments was a target of Roseanne's ire. Co-star Sarah Gilbert was to blame. The sleeping aid Ambien had something to do with it (Bakare, 2018). Executives at ABC whom she blasted for caving in to "political correctness." And of course, her "liberal" critics who were supposedly out to get her from the outset. For the record, the Ambien defense prompted the drug maker to issue a public statement with a deft level of wicked wit stating that "racism is not a known side effect." Hello! Drop the mic! Touchdown!

As a 65-year-old White woman, Barr should have known better. Moreover, being a White woman who is also Jewish, and is of an age where she is well aware of anti-Semitism, you would think she would have some degree of cultural sensitivity. If we are being honest with ourselves, she probably did. She probably assumed that she had been granted so many passes for previous brash and obnoxious behavior including her notorious bizarre national anthem performance at the 1990 San Diego Padres game almost three decades ago that she would be able to get away with her latest insult, which was a blatant racial affront to millions of people of African descent throughout the world. And get this, as if that was not insulting enough, with a straight face she had the gall to say that she thought Valarie Jarrett was White! Really Roseanne? Did you think we (meaning the Black community and woke non-Black folk) are that stupid!? Girl! Please! Bye!

In her delusional mindset, she likely assumed that any controversy would quickly subside and everything would return to business as usual. After all, President Trump was a fan of both her and the show. She had an intense, dedicated fan base (Wright, 2018). She had made numerous cryptic comments in the past and suffered no severe backlash, why would she do so now? Well, it seemed that karma caught up with the acid-tongued comedian.

As many pundits and consultants from all walks of life and across the political spectrum have argued, and rightly so, ABC knew what they were getting when they entered into a partnership with Barr (Madison, 2018). It was not as if they were blindsided by a new up-and-coming novice who suddenly threw them a curve ball. Roseanne Barr is a veteran Hollywood celebrity who is known for her crude, crass, acerbic, frequently volatile disposition (Loofbourow, 2018). She is brash, foul mouthed, routinely belligerent, and embodies a take-no-prisoner persona. She does not hesitate to engage in vicious battles with everyone and anyone on social media. Hurling intense insults and being rude is her stock and trade. She's a loose cannon (Sims, 2018). Ms. Manners, she is not.

ABC saw Rosanne Barr as a potential cash cow, and rightly so. Ratings for her new series were record-breaking. Indeed, Barr garnered the type of ratings that are a dream for advertisers and network executives. People were probably hugging one another in the halls and popping champagne bottles at ABC the day after the ratings were announced. Hell, even President Trump weighed in on the issue, congratulating her for her impressive return to television. Her show spoke to a demographic that loves to see themselves in prime-time television.

To be sure, there were some on the conservative and cultural right, among them Ted Nugent and conspiracy theorist Alex Jones, millions of right-wing bloggers and others, who engaged in mental gymnastics, 'whataboutisms', and other baseless defenses, decrying what they saw as "double standards," political correctness, and other predictable language that usually emanate from right-wing circles when they perceive themselves as being under attack from outside forces (Trombetta, 2018). Mind you, this was the same Ted Nugent who referred to Hillary Clinton as a c*nt (as did many other of his right-wing cohorts) and unabashedly attacked President Obama and former First Lady Michelle Obama and their daughters, leveling the most shameless sort of scurrilous comments and accusations. The hypocrisy from a large segment of the right was shameless and disgraceful (Thomsen, 2018).

Some observers weighed in on the fact that Black women were involved in all aspects of this dramatic spectacle. Channing Dungey, Valarie Jarrett, and Susan Rice all are Black women. Strong, intelligent, professional, successful, powerful Black women. Each has a level of visibility and social status that cannot be ignored or minimized, even by those who would rather obscure their accomplishments. This fact in and of itself is both noteworthy and admirable.

Paranoia, hypocrisy, dishonesty, and symbolism aside, the truth is that with her attacks on Jarrett and previous attack on another Black woman, Roseanne engaged in the most heinous act of inflammatory racial rhetoric possible. Her comments were an insult to Jarrett, Black people, and decent human beings in general. Thank goodness ABC had the integrity to make the right decision in removing Barr from all aspects of the series, including the revised version of the series.

REFERENCES

Acuna, Kirsten (2018, June 21). A Roseanne spin-off is coming to ABC without "Roseanne" called "The Conners". *Culture*. Retrieved from https://www.thisisinsider.com/roseanne-spin-off-the-conners-abc-2018-6

Bakare, Lanre (2018, May 30). Roseanne Barr blames racist tweet on sleeping pills. *The Guardian*. Retrieved from https://www.theguardian.com/culture/2018/may/30/roseanne-barr-blames-racist-tweet-on-sleeping-pills

Koblin, John (2018, May 28) After racist tweet, Roseanne Barr's show is cancelled by ABC. *New York Times*. https://www.nytimes.com/2018/05/29/business/media/roseanne-barr-offensive-tweets.html

Madison, Ira (2018, May 29). ABC gave Roseanne Barr's racism a megaphone. What did it expect? *The Daily Beast*. Retrieved from https://www.thedailybeast.com/abc-gave-roseanne-barrs-racism-a-megaphone-what-did-it-expect

Martin, Garrett (2018, May 29). Hey ABC, Roseanne never should've returned in the first place. *Paste*. Retrieved from https://www.pastemagazine.com/articles/2018/05/roseanne-twitter.html

May, Ashley (2018, May 30). Ambien Maker to Roseanne: Racism is not a side effect of our drug. *USA Today*. Retrieved from https://eu.usatoday.com/story/news/nation-now/2018/05/30/roseanne-barr-blames-ambien-zolpidem-drug-real-side-effects/654683002/

Sims, David (2018, May 29). Why ABC finally had to cancel Roseanne. *The Atlantic*. Retrieved from https://www.theatlantic.com/entertainment/archive/2018/05/abc-cancels-roseanne-barr/561461/

Thomsen, Jacqueline (2018, May 31). Chelsea Clinton resurfaces Trump meeting with Ted Nugent who once called Hillary C-word. *The Hill*. Retrieved from https://thehill.com/blogs/in-the-know/in-the-know/390118-chelsea-clinton-resurfaces-trump-meeting-with-ted-nugent-who

Trombetta, Sadie (2018, June 1). The difference between Roseanne Barr's overt racism and Samantha Bee's crude remark. *Hello Giggles*. Retrieved from https://hellogiggles.com/news/difference-between-roseanne-racism-samantha-bee/

Wright, Jennifer (2018, May 31). Roseanne Barr succeeded because of her backward views: Not in spite of them. *Harper's Bazaar*. Retrieved from https://www.harpersbazaar.com/culture/politics/a20968159/roseanne-barr-racist-tweet/

Public Statement from ABC News Entertainment President Channing Dungey. (2018, May 29).

38

Aretha Franklin: Feminist, Activist, Phenomenal Woman

On August 16, 2018, the world lost one of the greatest singers of all time. Aretha Louise Franklin, the Memphis-born, Detroit-raised singer passed away at the age of 76. Franklin had one of the most distinguished voices ever. For more than half a century, her music etched itself into popular culture as readily as the air we breathe and the water we drink (Myers, 2018). For many of us, her music was an essential part of our lives. Her songs nourished our minds, souls, and body. After all, she was indeed the "Queen of Soul!"

Aretha made you move, jump, snap your fingers, move your shoulders, bob your head, and shuffle your feet. In short, your entire body was invigorated at some level when Ms. Franklin sang. Indeed, I am one who sang out loud when listening to her music. You could dance to "Freeway of Love," feel the intense authenticity of "Ain't No Way," or get your sensual groove on with "Baby I Love You" and "Dr. Feelgood." My personal favorite was "Angel." Aretha knew how to touch your emotions (Graham, 2018). For some of us, listening to her music was like going to church.

In 1967, millions of American women cheered when she powerfully belted out the words R-E-S-P-E-C-T. Her vocal performance was so dynamic and powerful. "Respect" was originally recorded by Otis Redding. Redding's song discussed how a woman should respond to and treat the man in her life (Brown, 2018). However, Franklin, with an undeniable maturity and unrestrained confidence, took Redding's message, went on the offense, and produced a revised version that became both a feminist and civil rights anthem (Joseph, 2018). The song became a classic. After hearing Aretha's version, Redding joked, "That girl stole my song."

Aretha grew up in Detroit's New Bethel Baptist Church, where her father, the legendary C. L. Franklin delivered powerful, in some cases, gut-wrenching sermons from the pulpit. More than a few people believe that she adopted her father's unflinching style in the manner that she sang. The young Aretha had the good fortune to grow up in an environment under the shadow of some of the most prominent Black singers and clergy of the mid-twentieth century. Dinah Washington, and the legendary Mahalia Jackson (my grandmother's favorite singer) and others were frequent visitors to the Franklin home and church. There is strong reason to assume that being in the presence of such strong, impervious, Black women like Lena Horne, Hazel Scott, Odetta Holmes accounted for her unapologetic and fierce commitment to the cause of social justice in all its forms (Riley, 2018).

This was evident in 1970 when Aretha offered to post bail for Angela Davis, who at the time, was a member of the communist party, and had been charged with conspiracy, kidnapping, and murder. Others advised her to avoid any association or interaction with Davis, who was seen by many people, including Aretha's father (who like others was understandably concerned about potential repercussions for his daughter's career), as too controversial. Despite such warnings from friends and allies (Griffin, 2018), Franklin ignored the naysayers and voiced strong support for Davis and offered to post her bail which was $250,000. Ultimately, she was unable to post bail for Davis due to the fact that she was traveling abroad at the time. Davis' bail was posted by Rodger McAfee, a White California dairy farmer who harbored left-wing political views.

While not overtly political, Franklin was astute to the power of her platform and used her voice for more than just belting out songs and entertaining audiences. She was a proud and strong advocate for the Black community, in particular, Black women. She employed her feminist activism sensibilities in a manner that produced real, concrete results. Unlike some artists of color who tried to walk a middle line in an effort to not offend White sensibilities, she comfortably luxuriated in her authentic Blackness in both her music and activism, and did not apologize for it (Watson, 2018). With Aretha Franklin, the intersection of race and gender was real (Newkirk, 2018).

From the late 1960s up until the mid-1970s, she was a perennial force in the music industry and frequently dominated the charts and award shows. By the mid-1970s, her career cooled off somewhat and other Black female singers such as Roberta Flack, Freda Payne, Donna Summer, and others were becoming equally popular with the public. The standstill was short lived as she ferociously rebounded in the mid-1980s with chart topping hits such as "Freeway of Love," "Jump To It," and "I Knew You'd Be Waiting for Me," with the late George Michael. In later years, she was a routine presence at many significant venues. She performed for three US presidents and sang for Pope Francis in 2015. Who can forget her spellbinding, tour de force performance that bought the house down at the 2015 Kennedy Center Honors where she sang her iconic "You Make Me Feel Like a Natural Woman," as she paid tribute to Carole King.

Yes, there will be future singers and performers endowed with exceptional talent, but the undisputed truth is that Aretha Franklin was one of a kind. As I see it, there will never be another performer like her. On June 30, 2018, she was laid to rest (Lartley, 2018). The sounds of heaven are a lot more soulful now as Aretha sings with her new angelic family. Rest in peace Ms. Franklin.

REFERENCES

Brown, DeNeen L. (2018, August 16). How Aretha Franklin's 'Respect' became an anthem for civil rights and feminism. *The Washington Post*. Retrieved from https://www.washingtonpost.com/news/retropolis/wp/2018/08/14/how-aretha-franklins-respect-became-an-anthem-for-civil-rights-and-feminism/

Garcia, Sandra (2018, August 17). Aretha Franklin, civil rights stalwart in her voice, we could feel our history. *New York Times*. Retrieved from https://www.nytimes.com/2018/08/17/arts/aretha-franklin-dead-civil-rights.html

Graham, Renee (2018, August 16). All praise is due to the Queen of Soul. *Boston Globe*. Retrieved from https://www.bostonglobe.com/opinion/2018/08/16/all-praises-due-queen-soul/O7UOhUpFMpFJVit8Bu4SnN/story.html

Griffin, Farah (2018, August 16). Aretha Franklin — Musical genius, truth teller, freedom fighter. *The Nation*. Retrieved from https://www.thenation.com/article/aretha-franklin-musical-genius-truth-teller-freedom-fighter/

Joseph, Yvette (2018, August 18). Aretha Franklin was the personification of black woman magic. *New York Times*. Retrieved from https://www.nytimes.com/2018/08/18/arts/music/aretha-franklin-black-women.html

Lartley, Jamiles (2018, August 30). Aretha Franklin: Friends, family and stars say goodbye to the Queen of Soul. *The Guardian*. Retrieved from https://theworldnews.net/gb-news/aretha-franklin-friends-family-and-stars-say-goodbye-to-the-queen-of-soul

Myers, Marc (2018, August 16). Aretha Franklin the Queen of Soul, dies. *Wall Street Journal*. Retrieved from https://www.wsj.com/articles/aretha-franklin-the-queen-of-soul-dies-1534428283

Newkirk, Vann (2018, August 16). Aretha Franklin's revolution. *The Atlantic*. Retrieved from https://www.theatlantic.com/entertainment/archive/2018/08/aretha-franklins-revolution/567715

Riley, Rochelle (2018, August 15). Jesse Jackson on Aretha Franklin's quiet but profound civil rights legacy. *Detroit Free Press*. Retrieved from https://eu.freep.com/story/news/columnists/rochelle-riley/2018/08/15/aretha-franklin-civil-rights-detroit/996436002/

Watson, Elwood (2018, August 19). Aretha Franklin, feminist and activist. *The Washington Post*. Retrieved from https://www.washingtonpost.com/news/made-by-history/wp/2018/08/19/aretha-franklin-feminist-and-activist/?noredirect=on&utm_term=.36f0a8c5eefd

39

Omarosa, Donald Trump, and Unalloyed Racial Bullhorns

From Steve Bannon, Michael Cohen, Corey Lewandowski, Anthony Scara-mucci, Sean Spicer, Omarosa Manigault Newman, one thing is for certain, Donald Trump sure knows how to pick em! With the release of Omarosa's book, *Unhinged: An Insiders Account of the Trump White House*, which was released in August 2018, the periodic reality television star, D list celebrity, former senior White House Trump staffer, and occasional nemesis of the president set all avenues of the print, mainstream, and electronic media abuzz with titillating, salacious, and outright morbid allegations about specific former staff members, various White House officials, and, of course, the current commander-in-chief himself, President Trump.

All of the cable outlets, MSNBC, CNN, FOX News (yes FOX News), as well as high-brow publications, *New York Times*, *The Atlantic*, *Wall Street Journal*, etc. and other mainstream publications wasted no time in report-ing the numerous number of scurrilous accusations and allegations levied by Ms. Manigault-Newman. Most notably, the president's supposed mental instability and racism (Guida, 2018).

The reaction from many political quarters ranged from shock, anger, cyni-cism, and amusement to, in some cases, outright and profound disgust. Trump detractors and others on the left were not exactly surprised by the revelations however. On the political right, many have taken aim at the messenger, Omarosa herself (Joondeph, 2018). She was attacked and derided as disingenuous, opportunistic, irrational, and to the title of her book — *Unhinged*.

Being the media-savvy hound that she is, Omarosa wasted no time in saturating radio and television, releasing tapes (Colvin & Lucy, 2018), and levying serious allegations about the president and many former co-workers. Her interview with *Meet the Press* host, Chuck Todd, that covered many issues, including the allegation that Trump used the word "nigger" was nothing short of riveting (Todd, 2018).

Like many people, I have taken some degree of interest in the dramatic episodes that frequently emanate from this disturbingly tumultuous admin-istration. One particularly engaging article written by Elaina Plott went into tedious detail exposing how Omarosa referred to several of her colleagues (Plott, 2018): Vice President Mike Pence was ambitious, scheming, and disciplined. Hope Hicks was described as friendly, capable, sensitive, out of her depth. Reince Priebus was a likable but weak person. Sean Spicer was nervous and highly strung.

Unsurprisingly, the reaction from the White House has been anything but positive. Dispute about the book was not confined to just the White House GOP pollster Frank Luntz and White House press secretary Sarah Huckabee Sanders, who have intensely disputed the book's claims, Trump took to Twitter denouncing her as "shameless," "opportunistic," and "wacky," "crazed," "unqualified," and other unflattering terms. The fact that Donald Trump took to social media to attack his former friend and supposed confi-dante was hardly surprising. What did raise more than a few eyebrows was when Trump referred to Ms. Manigault Newman as a "dog." Yep! You read it correctly. The president of the United States referred to his former employee, a Black woman, as a dog!

Let's just cut to the chase, this is nothing short of outrageous. Need-less to say, Black Twitter, vast segments of Black America (and people of all races and ethnicities) became lit and rightly so (Timpf, 2018). This is nothing but vehement, sexist, racist rhetoric of the most odious kind. Moreover, it fits a disturbing pattern of a president who has routinely targeted and attacked Black people (Don Lemon, Maxine Waters, LeBron James, Frederica Wilson, etc.) and others, questioning their intelligence and humanity. Seeing them as less than human. The fact that White House press secretary Sarah Huckabee Sanders could not definitively confirm that there are no tapes where the president had used the N-word spoke volumes.

In fact, this is common fare among racists to historically refer to Black people as apes, monkeys, dogs, and in other grossly unflattering terms equat-ing people of color with animals. Such attitudes are as old as the nation itself, and there are Whites who concede this fact. In the comment section of the

New York Times, one subscriber who used his full name posted a comment stating:

> *Trump can call a black person "dog" or much worse, and in so doing he is expressing what many whites feel but cannot openly say. As a white older male, I can't even count the times I hear whites refer to blacks in demeaning terms. In fact, black people have no idea how prevalent it is among whites of any social standing to think of blacks as lesser humans. What Trump is doing is allowing whites to own their racism and ignorance with pride.*
>
> — Richard Monckton, San Francisco, California

While Mr. Monckton's post is largely spot on, I would challenge him on his assumption that Black people are unaware of how many White people see them as fully less than human. The reality is that a sizable number of Black people are aware of this.

The majority of Black people (and a good number of other non-Whites for that matter, especially those over 45 and older) are not under any illusion that the overwhelming majority of White people harbor a "we are the world" "he ain't heavy, he's my brother," disposition when it comes to their attitudes toward non-Whites. History has demonstrated otherwise.

Truth be told, I (like many people) have never been a fan of Omarosa for varied and obvious reasons — her perverse arrogance, shameless opportunism, mean-spirited persona, frequently juvenile behavior and largely devious personality among them. Quite frankly, any reasonable person should take the allegations she has made with utmost caution. Moreover, she has been complicit in all the nefarious activities of the president and adopted many of his values (O'Brien, 2018), until she was cast aside and kicked off the elite reservation. On the contrary, given her unusual relationship with Trump, she may be playing most of us for suckers. That being said, it is totally unacceptable and irresponsible for the president to refer to any woman, regardless of race, in this manner (Joondeph, 2018). It is the height of racism and misogyny.

Trump is far from an inspiring president. While he has a base that is imperviously loyal to him and is highly unlikely to abandon him regardless of how crass, crude, and obscene he is, the deafening silence of so many mainstream Republicans was both troubling and disturbing. Those dismissing his antics are even worse. One can only imagine what the reaction would be from the conservative right if former president Barack Obama had behaved in such a manner. There would have been immediate calls for impeachment.

I would like to think that most of us are astute enough to realize that a White House where drama flows like a river at high tide and encompasses a Hemingway level of dysfunction does no good to its inhabitants, its leaders, its nation's citizens, and the nation itself. Something has to give. Nonetheless, Omarosa, the chaotic, obsessive personality that she is, had no problem taking advantage of similarly dysfunctional people and profited handsomely off the Trump havoc-wreaking train (Stephens, 2018).

REFERENCES

Colvin, Jill, & Lucy, Catherine (2018, August 13). Omarosa release's another recording, this one features Trump himself. *Truthdig*. Retrieved from https://www.truthdig.com/articles/omarosa-releases-another-recording-this-one-featuring-trump-himself/

Guida, Victor (2018, August 12). Trump is mentally declined. *Politico*. Retrieved from https://www.politico.com/story/2018/08/12/omarosa-trump-mental-state-book-kelly-773889

Joondeph, Brian (2018, August 17). Trump and Omarosa. *American Thinker*. Retrieved from https://www.americanthinker.com/articles/2018/08/trump_and_omarosa.html

Newman, Omarosa Manigault (2018). *Unhinged: An insider's account of the Trump White House*. New York: Gallery Books.

O'Brien, Timothy (2018, August 13). Trump and Omarosa are kindred spirits. *Bloomberg Opinion*. Retrieved from https://www.bloomberg.com/opinion/articles/2018-08-13/trump-and-omarosa-are-kindred-spirits

Omarosa's interview with Chuck Todd (2018, August 12). *NBC*. Retrieved from https://www.nbcnews.com/meet-the-press/meet-press-august-12-2018-n899996

Plott, Elaine (2018, August 13). What Omarosa thinks of Pence, Melania and the Trump kids? *The Atlantic*. Retrieved from https://www.scribd.com/article/386142567/What-Omarosa-Thinks-Of-Pence-Melania-And-The-Trump-Kids

Ralph, Pat (2018, August 14) Sarah Huckabee Sanders gets grilled in press briefing about Omarosa's fiery new book, *Business Insider*. Retrieved from https://www.businessinsider.com/white-house-press-briefing-omarosa-book-2018-8

Stephens, Bret (2018, August 16). This is your brain on Omarosa. *New York Times*. Retrieved from https://www.nytimes.com/2018/08/16/opinion/omarosa-trump-afghanistan.html

Timpf, Katherine (2018, August 14). Trump might as well be paying Omarosa again. *National Review*. Retrieved from https://www.nationalreview.com/2018/08/trump-spat-giving-omarosa-manigault-attention-book-sales/

40

Why Is the Conservative Right So Obsessed with Alexandria Ocasio-Cortez?

Alexandria Ocasio-Cortez's interview with CNN journalist and 60 Minutes correspondent Anderson Cooper on January 3, 2019 where she stated that she believed President Trump was a racist caused a considerable buzz across the political spectrum. Her comments garnered applause from the political left and rampant condemnation from the political right. Max Boot, conservative CNN political pundit, self-described Never-Trumper and columnist for the *Washington Post*, wrote an extremely cynical article comparing the young vibrant congresswoman to Sarah Palin (Boot, 2019). Yes, you read that correctly. He sees Ms. Ocasio-Cortez as strikingly similar to the former Alaska governor and Vice Presidential candidate.

Such an analogy is nonsensical. The truth is that Ocasio-Cortez is (at least not yet) nothing like the rogue Ms. Palin. On the contrary, she is largely the antithesis of former Alaska governor and 2008 GOP vice presidential candidate. One can only wonder what it is that has caused (at least for the time being) so many conservatives to have such a rabid fixation with this young Hispanic woman. Indeed, the level of scrutiny directed toward her among the right has reached the point of frenzy.

In early 2019, right before she was sworn in as a newly elected freshman congresswoman, one of her right-wing detractors decided to locate a video of Ocasio-Cortez dancing and post it on social media. The video, which can be seen on YouTube and other social media platforms, showcased the New York City politician showing off her lucid hoofing skills (for some of you younger readers, hoofing means dancing) while she was a student at Boston University. Suffice to say, that girlfriend could move!

Apparently, the assumption was that somehow such a video of a young college girl dancing (fully clothed I might add) would supposedly shame the very popular congresswoman. Needless to say the strategy backfired, and was attacked and roundly, soundly, viciously, and justifiably condemned by various corners of the political, social, and cultural left (Shamsian, 2019). On the contrary, it actually garnered Ocasio-Cortez more fans and further endeared her to the large number of supporters that she already had (Cherelus, 2019).

Rather than go on the defensive, the seemingly ever ready, savvy Ocasio-Cortez responded in her usual proactive manner, took to Twitter and went on an elegant offense with her most recent dancing video. She even played the classic Edwin Starr song "War," danced in the halls of congress, and promptly closed her office door (Reiman, 2019), effectively telling her critics to get lost, and that she has work to do.

However, this did not deter some of her right-wing critics from continuing in their sinister efforts to publically humiliate Ocasio-Cortez. Assuming they had finally nailed her and "had the goods" so-to-speak, a few newspapers posted an online image of what was supposed to be a nude photo of the congresswoman. Guess what? The photo was fake. Her enemies were busted again (Pilkington, 2019). Understandably, she lashed out at those behind the botched effort to humiliate her. Once again, her conservative critics were forced to eat crow, and wipe the raw eggs off their frustrated faces.

Ever since the Bronx congresswoman won a stunning victory in the summer of 2018 over her much more well-known and financed opponent, Ocasio-Cortez has been the subject of intense interest from wide swaths of the American public. While she has become a darling of the progressive left, she has been routinely vilified, crucified, and largely despised by many conservatives (Valenti, 2019). To say that the conservative right is obsessed with Alexandria Ocasio-Cortez is a major understatement. To right-wing conservatives, she is public enemy number one. Satan's sister, lady from hell, and so forth.

Irascible and "Black people are always causing problems" conservative radio host, Ben Shapiro, seems to be in Ocasio-Cortez mode on a regular basis. He cannot let a week go by without commenting on her. In fact, his fascination with the young millennial congressperson is so intense that he eagerly challenged her to a debate. She deftly and shrewdly declined his dubious request (Fenwick, 2019).

Shapiro is not alone. *The National Review*, the now defunct *Weekly Standard*, Breitbart.com, and other mainstream conservative publications have written at length about her. Some staff members at the more politically far-right publications probably have rabid nightmares about her. One thing is for certain, she is living rent free in many of their minds and has infested herself deep into the darkest corners of their psyches (McLaughlin, 2019).

There are a number of reasons that right-wing obsession with her is so rampant. For one, she is an avowed leftist politician from the progressive wing of the Democratic Party. She is a woman of color and one of a minute number of Latina women in congress. She is intelligent and she is attractive. She is unapologetic and combative in a professional sense (Pollitt, 2019).

She is also, at 29 years old, the youngest person ever to be elected to congress. Young, Latina, politically progressive, has supermodel looks, and exudes an unabashed, refreshing level of confidence. She is a living nightmare for many right-wingers, representing almost everything they dislike (Serwer, 2019).

To be honest, even some of her fellow democrats are rankled by her intense ferocity. However, if anything, her fellow democratic congressmen need to take a page, or a few pages for that matter, from her playbook. For a first-term congressperson to have struck such fear into a sizable sector of a political movement is extremely interesting. She literally terrifies them (Osterheldt, 2019).

To be frank, I think there is a segment of conservative men who secretly have a crush on her and resent themselves for it. They are in denial about their sexual admiration for her. They disguise it.

Alexandria Ocasio-Cortez along with Rashida Tlaib, Jahana Hayes, Grace Merg, Ilhan Oman, Yvette Clarke, Ayanna Pressley, Lauren Underwood, Veronica Escobar, Brenda Lawrence, Sharice Davis, Debra Haaland, and others were among a number of women of color to be elected to congress in 2018. As of this moment, Ms. Ocasio-Cortez (although Rashida Tlaib is beginning to make some waves) seems to be the woman of color who is most effectively the boat of the establishment.

She is brave. She is bold. She is sassy. She is competent. She is a multiple threat. Let's hope that other sisters of color will begin to help her rock and row the boat as well.

REFERENCES

Boot, Max (2015, January 8). Alexandria Ocasio-Cortez shouldn't approach her facts the way Trump does. *The Washington Post*. Retrieved from https://www.washingtonpost.com/opinions/2019/01/08/alexandria-ocasio-cortez-shouldnt-approach-her-facts-way-trump-does/

Cherelus, Gina (2019, January 4). Dance-off: Attempt to shame Ocasio-Cortez with video backfires. *U.S News & World Report*. Retrieved from https://www.usnews.com/news/top-news/articles/2019-01-04/dance-off-attempt-to-shame-ocasio-cortez-with-video-backfires

Fenwick, Cody (2019, August 10). Alexandria Ocasio-Cortez perfectly shuts down Ben Shapiro's pesky challenge to debate. *Salon*. Retrieved from https://www.salon.com/2018/08/10/alexandria-ocasio-cortez-shuts-down-ben-shapiro-and-his-calls-for-a-debate_partner/

Huertas, Aaron (2019, January 18). What democrats can learn from Alexandria Ocasio-Cortez? *Medium*. Retrieved from https://medium.com/s/story/democrats-should-be-learning-from-alexandria-ocasio-cortezs-communications-style-not-dismissing-9b9bd0c24dc3

McLaughlin, Dan (2019, January 4). Why does Alexandria Ocasio-Cortez get so much attention from the Right? *National Review*. Retrieved from https://www.nationalreview.com/corner/why-does-alexandria-ocasio-cortez-get-so-much-attention-from-the-right/

Osterheldt, Jenee (2019, January 11). New party, who dis?' Alexandria Ocasio-Cortez has everybody shook. *Boston Globe*. Retrieved from https://www.bostonglobe.com/metro/2019/01/11/new-party-who-dis-alexandria-ocasio-cortez-has-everybody-shook/fV51IWlj4ulGi5Swf1hiBM/story.html

Pilkington, Ed (2019, January 9). Alexandria Ocasio-Cortez hits out at disgusting media publishing fake nude image. *The Guardian*. Retrieved from https://www.theguardian.com/us-news/2019/jan/10/alexandria-ocasio-cortez-hits-out-at-disgusting-media-publishing-fake-nude-image

Pollitt, Katha (2019, January 10). The end of likability politics. *The Nation*. Retrieved from https://www.thenation.com/article/aoc-tlaib-warren-womens-march/

Reiman, Eliza (2019, January 4). Alexandria Ocasio-Cortez responds to conservatives who criticized her dancing in college with a new video of her dancing outside her office. *Business Insider*. Retrieved from https://www.businessinsider.com/alexandria-ocasio-cortez-responds-conservative-critics-new-dancing-video-2019-1?r=US&IR=T

Serwer, Adam (2019, January 9). The exception to the rulers. *The Atlantic*. Retrieved from https://www.theatlantic.com/ideas/archive/2019/01/why-conservatives-cant-stop-talking-about-alexandria-ocasio-cortez/579901/

Shamsian, Jacob (2019, January 3). People are making fun of conservatives for criticizing Alexandria Ocasio-Cortez's dancing. *Insider Politics*. Retrieved from https://www.thisisinsider.com/video-alexandria-ocasio-cortez-dancing-backfire-critics-2019-1

Valenti, Jessica (2019, January 10). Who's afraid of AOC? *Medium*. Retrieved from https://medium.com/s/jessica-valenti/whos-afraid-of-aoc-ba3ac04d28b3

41

R. Kelly and the Ongoing Disregard, Devaluation, Denigration and Degradation of Black Women

In January 2019, law enforcement in Chicago and Atlanta began looking into accusations that R&B singer Robert Kelly (better known as R. Kelly) was engaging in lewd, intense, graphic sexual activity with numerous underage teenage girls in both cities over a two-decade period (Coscarelli, 2019). Such investigations came after Lifetime television aired the docu-series *Surviving R. Kelly*. The several-part series was a riveting, heartbreaking saga that chronicled the experiences of dozens of women, a number of whom were teenagers and, in some cases, pre-pubescent girls at the time such sex acts took place. The critically acclaimed documentary is a must-see series for all those concerned about the sexual abuse of women and children, in particular, young Black women and girls.

Reaction to the series was passionate and heated. Americans across the racial, social, economic, gender, and political spectrum, as well as citizens all over the world, were captivated by the cascade of riveting and sordid allegations levied against the music superstar. This was certainly the case with Black Americans. Certain celebrities who had previously remained mum on such nefarious activities for years, and in some cases, decades, suddenly "saw the light" and found the courage to speak out against R. Kelly. Lady Gaga, Nick Cannon, Chance the Rapper, Celine Dion, and Pussycat Dolls were just a few who initially took to the airwaves issuing belated mea culpas expressing regret for collaborating with the accused and alleged sexual predator (Lockett and Rothstein, 2019).

For their part, both Mr. Kelly and his team of attorneys immediately issued steadfast denials in regards to the charges (Babwin, 2019). Indeed, Kelly's attorney, Steve Greenberg brashly dismissed Kelly's accusers labeling them as "grudge holding, leeching, disappointed opportunists" who latched on to his client yet became disgruntled and resentful when the careers they hoped for failed to materialize. In essence, Mr. Greenberg aggressively employed the "hell hath no fury like an ambitious and disappointed scorned woman" defense.

While troubling, one can likely understand why Kelly's legal team reacted like barbarians at the gate, rushing to defend him. He was/is their livelihood, meal ticket, and financial repository. Having R. Kelly weakened or indicted would result in the disruption of their financial pocketbooks. Thus, he had to be protected at all costs, no matter how vile, untoward, and unethical it was for them to do so.

Unsurprisingly (at least for those of us whose eyes and ears are glued to Black popular culture) a notable segment of the Black community has been supportive of R. Kelly or is at the very least ambivalent about the slew of scurrilous allegations levied against the R&B musician. These are the men (and more than a few women) who indulge in the "they are trying to bring another powerful Black man down" argument.

As was the case with other Black men who have been accused and, in some cases, indicted for nefarious behavior, these are the supposedly racially conscious, "down with the cause" astute Black folk who view Kelly as being the unfair and tragic victim of manufactured, trumped up, if not outright false charges, whipped up by powerful subversive elements determined to see another Black man destroyed (Hill, 2019). And guess what? They have recruited hundreds of lying Black women along the way, secretly gave some of them chump change, and provided serious cash to others under the table. My response to such derelict, conspiratorial thinking is "negroes please, I don't think so."

It has been this sort of complicity and willful denial from many segments of the Black community that has enabled R. Kelly and others of his ilk to escape any sort of punishment for their sinister, pathological behavior and only later to face a form of watered down, belated justice or suffer no consequences at all for their actions (Grundy, 2019). The undisputed truth is that fans of all races, the media, and the music industry were all too willing to adopt a "hear no evil, see no evil, fear no evil" philosophy when it came to R. Kelly. Some still are for that matter.

In fact, *Chicago Sun Times* reporter, Jim De Rogatis was the first reporter who exposed the singer's alleged pursuit and abuse of underage girls (Goldstein, 2018). Rather than being taken seriously De Rogatis was largely relegated to a voice in the wilderness for the better part of two decades. This fact in and of itself is outrageous and disturbing.

If we are being frank about it (and I am), sad to say, the words of Black women are often given short shrift in our society. Simply put, Black women are not given the benefit of the doubt that their White female counterparts are. They are members of a culture and society that views them as wanton juvenile, suspect, devious, rapacious, and so on. Media depictions of Black women as loudmouthed, combative, untrustworthy, sassy, hip-holding, eye-rolling, and trash-talking sapphires have dominated the television landscape for decades. Do images of Omarosa, Diamond and Silk, Ne Ne Leakes, *Housewives of Atlanta*, etc. come to mind? (Watson, 2013).

Let me make it clear. I am well aware of the fact that Black men and Black people in general have been the victims of rampant injustices. Given our history, one can understand why more than a few Black Americans proceed with caution when hearing about the supposed transgressions of one of our own from outside sources, particularly when the person in question is a beloved, powerful, and successful individual like R. Kelly. With so many suffering from drug abuse, skyrocketing rates of mental illness, in prison, unemployed or underemployed, success stories like Kelly's provided a glimmer of hope onto a racial landscape that is often far too bleak when it comes to Black men.

Protection and pride aside, the fact is that we should not and cannot support the sexual violation of women of any race. Period. If such accusations are, in fact, true, then a major injustice has been perpetrated on these young women even if many of them are now fully-grown adults. Some of them were likely the victims of pedophilia. These women deserve justice.

The silence among too many in the Black community, especially Black men, has been nothing short of deafening. It is as if these young ladies are not worthy of any level of human dignity (Graham, 2018). Malcolm X expressed it best in a 1962 speech, "The most disrespected person in America is the black woman. The most unprotected person in America is the Black woman. The most neglected person in America is the black woman" (Malcolm X, 1962).

We have seen this play out time-and-time again from the days of slavery, the mid-twentieth century during the days of Jim Crow and the civil rights movement. Such intra-racial divisive drama manifested itself during the Anita Hill/Clarence Thomas hearings. We are witnessing such brazen animosity here in the present day where Black female journalists are routinely disregarded and disrespected by President Trump. More than a half a century later, Malcolm X's words still ring true.

Black women have been the backbone of the Black race. They have done so with undeniable credibility, and have kept our people above water. Historically, Black women have come to the aid of Black men, White women (ask Hilary Clinton in 2016 and Doug Jones in Alabama in 2017), and pretty much everyone else, yet the same level of support and loyalty from others is rarely, if ever, reciprocated (Milloy, 2018). Their formidable tenacity and fierce strength have been nothing short of herculean. Such continued disloyalty and betrayal from others must change. There is no other way to say it, Black women deserve better (Emba, 2019). Period.

REFERENCES

Babwin, Don (2019, January 11). Lawyer: R. Kelly denies all sexual misconduct allegations. *Associated Press*. Retrieved from https://www.washingtontimes.com/news/2019/jan/11/lawyer-r-kelly-denies-all-sexual-misconduct-allega/

Coscarelli, Joe (2019, January 8). Investigators looking into accusations from R. Kelly documentary. *New York Times*. Retrieved from https://www.nytimes.com/2019/01/08/arts/music/r-kelly-criminal-investigation.html

Emba, Christine (2019, January 9). Black women deserve better. *The Washington Post*. Retrieved from https://www.washingtonpost.com/opinions/black-women-deserve-better-will-2019-be-the-year-of-change/2019/01/09/fc40e842-1439-11e9-803c-4ef28312c8b9_story.html

Goldstein, Jessica (2018, May 14). The reporter who broke the R. Kelly story is ready for everyone else to care about it. *Think Progress*. Retrieved from https://thinkprogress.org/rkelly-reporter-wants-your-attention-6de8bd8cd0fe/

Graham, Renee (2018, May 15). Black women are waiting for their #Me Too moment. *Boston Globe*. Retrieved from https://www.bostonglobe.com/opinion/2018/05/15/black-women-are-waiting-for-their-metoo-moment/BuZ8Q-JXP09k6ZNKIDgdTBJ/story.html

Grundy, Saida (2019, January 10). The flawed logic of R. Kelly's most unlikely supporters. *The Atlantic*. Retrieved from https://www.theatlantic.com/entertainment/archive/2019/01/why-some-women-still-support-r-kelly/579985/

Hill, Jemele (2019, January 11). R. Kelly and the cost of black protectionism. *The Atlantic*. Retrieved from https://www.theatlantic.com/entertainment/archive/2019/01/r-kelly-and-cost-black-protectionism/580150/

Lockett, De, & Rothstein, Katie (2019, January 15). All the artists who denounced R. Kelly. *Vulture*. Retrieved from https://www.vulture.com/2019/02/artists-issue-r-kelly-apology-updated-list.html

Malcolm X Network (1962), *Archives*.

Milloy, Courtland (2018, November 13). Where are black men in the fight for black women? *The Washington Post*. Retrieved from https://www.washingtonpost.com/local/where-are-black-men-in-the-fight-for-black-women/2018/11/13/63030e0c-e771-11e8-a939-9469f1166f9d_story.html

Watson, Elwood (2013, January 17). Humiliation, ridicule of black women must end. *Diverse Education*. Retrieved from https://diverseeducation.com/article/50726/

Afterword

In November 1992, Queen Elizabeth II delivered a speech to the British public in London at Guildhall, describing the events that had affected the royal family that year. Throughout what was a very detailed speech, she specifically made the comment "1992 will not be a year that I will look back upon with undiluted pleasure. It has been an 'annus horrible.'" To be sure, 1992 was not exactly serene for the royal family, given the number of crises that plagued them that year — Princess Anne's divorce from Mark Phillips, the separations of Prince Charles and Princess Diana and the Duke and Duchess of York, and the ferocious fire that did tremendous damage to Windsor Castle. She was right on target in her remarks.

Now, more than a quarter of a century later, there has been much speculation about the past few years that have occurred in America, particularly since the mid-2010s. More than a few people have lamented that they feel the past few years have been among the worst in our nation's history. In fact, a considerable number of people argue that each successive year seems to be more dramatic than the previous one.

As a man who is still in early middle age, I honestly have to say that I cannot remember a time period that has been filled with as much tension, anxiety, and drama as the one we currently reside in. Whether it be continual and amplified unrest in the Middle East and North Korea. The drama occurring at the Mexican border. The non-stop level of police and other forms of violence routinely inflicted on Black and in some cases, Latino/a people. Dangerously hyper-political polarization. Fractured race relations. Enormous wealth gaps between different economic groups. Hate crimes against minority groups. Continued unrest on college campuses. Growing economic disparity and so on. Much of the past decade has been a challenging time on many fronts.

The truth is that America, throughout its young history (compared to most nations we are an infant), has dealt with significant crises such as the Revolutionary War, Civil War, Great Depression, World War II, just to name a few. For many people of color and other marginalized groups, the current period is just one of many of continual isolation and oppression. It is business as usual. No racially or socially conscious person can deny the fact that we are living in an unsettling moment of American history.

To say we are living in the worst of times is an argument that is certainly up for debate. For example:

- 1837 was the Trail of Tears that humiliated and decimated much of that Native American population.
- 1877 when Rutherford B. Hayes with the help of his vice president, Samuel Tilden, pulled union troops out of the South and officially ended Reconstruction prompting a wave of terror, humiliation, and discrimination against Black southerners (and Black people in other parts of the nation with slightly less severity) for more than 80 years.
- 1919 when high unemployment, massive labor strikes, and deadly bloody race riots dominated large pockets of the nation.
- 1968, the assassinations of Dr. Martin Luther King Jr. and Robert Kennedy in April and June of that year. The Democratic National Convention in Chicago where riots and civil unrest took place both inside the convention hall and out in the streets where cops battled it out with young people.
- 2003, where America managed to plunge itself into another war, further disrupting an already unstable Middle East region where the effects are still prevalent today.

The aforementioned events rattled the psyches and shook the souls of the individuals who resided in those respective eras.

More recently in the present, to add to the already gut-wrenching drama that has engulfed the current political environment, Justice Anthony Kennedy announced his resignation from the United States Supreme Court on June 27, 2018 (Shear, 2018). His announcement sent shock waves throughout the political world both in the Washington beltway and beyond (Mark, 2018). Reactions were swift and immediate.

Liberals and progressives responded with despair, angst, and disillusion. Conservatives reacted, in many cases, with unrestrained euphoria and cautious optimism.

On July 9, 2018, President Trump selected Brett Kavanaugh, currently a federal appeals judge for the District of Columbia, a fixture in conservative politics and widely respected by the Republican elite as his nominee to replace Anthony Kennedy. Such news was undoubtedly unnerving and dispiriting for many liberals and progressives, and euphoric for conservatives who have longed for decades to see the Supreme Court become a right-of-center majority in order to put its conservative stamp on the American legal system for generations. Kennedy was known as the swing vote on the current court, though he was hardly a reliable voice, in that he still voted with the court's conservative wing more often than not. This was particularly true with his final votes before stepping down from the court.

There are a number of social issues that hang in the balance with the nomination of Brett Kavanaugh, such as affirmative action, voting rights, reproductive rights, most notably the 1973 landmark decision Roe v. Wade (1973) rights of labor unions, privacy laws, gay marriage, campaign finance reform, higher education, and other issues that have long been important to the political and cultural left. Both sides of the political spectrum have vowed to charge forward in an effort to implement their agenda. Only time will tell if such concerns were justified.

The election of Donald Trump to the presidency in 2016 has overtones that are chillingly similar to the mid-nineteenth century. This was time when the talk of secession was becoming more and more commonplace among many states, particularly in the South. Moreover, Trump seems to revel in a rabid level of anti-intellectualism that would rival many Americans during the Jacksonian era of the early and mid-nineteenth century. More troubling, he has populated his forthcoming administration with some who are hostile to civil rights for non-Whites, reproductive rights and freedoms for women, marriage equality for gays and lesbians, support privatizing public education, climate change skeptics, disregard arguments made in supporting minimum wage salaries for employees, embrace virulently racist, sexist, homophobic, anti-Semitic, xenophobic, and other disgraceful values. Such actions should be alarming for anyone who harbors and advocates progressive and humane values for all citizens, including those who have been routinely and historically mistreated, devalued, and ostracized. In fact, many Americans feel that we are heading to another Civil War. The old saying, "history repeats itself" does sometimes ring true.

That being said, while many people on the left have prophesied that the election of Donald Trump will result in the end of liberalism, democracy, freedom, truth, hope, and other virtues traditionally associated with progressive and liberal values, I do not harbor such a dire and dramatic level of despair. I am well aware of the fact that this nation has undergone significant and monumental events — the Civil War, Great Depression, World War II etc. that would have sunk most other nations. Rather than implode, America survived, rebounded, and emerged even stronger after each catastrophe. Despite its flaws, the fact is that America is a feisty nation. Indeed, the spirit of America is one of strength and resilience in spite of all its controversies, and that includes race.

My motivation for writing this book is to revitalize the public conversation around the issue of race, despite the pessimism and staunch cynicism of a large segment of the American public. While we are living in an era where democracy seems to be under increasing attack with threats from both internal and external forces, I refuse to believe that all is lost. The fact is that this nation has been confronted with racial issues and milestones since the dawn of the republic. Slavery, the Civil War, Jim Crow, the Civil Rights Movement of the 1950s and 1960s, the election of the nation's first Black president in 2008. Each and every time, our nation has been forced to address the issue, no matter how reluctantly or awkwardly.

In a nation where all the demographic data indicates that non-Whites will be the majority by the mid-2040s, it is imperative that we begin to have frank, candid, uncensored conversations about one of America's most provocative issues — race. When Eric Holder, the first Black attorney general, made the comment that "Americans are cowards when it comes to discussing race" he was right on target (Barr, 2009).

While there has never been a grand moment for Black America, some argue that the 1960s was a Black renaissance of sorts, although I would argue that it was more a period of brief revolutionary activity that was met with violent resistance from various, unrelenting forces of White supremacy at every turn. The history of Blacks in America has always been one of one-step forward, two-steps backward. Whatever gains that were secured by law were often overshadowed or mitigated by larger oppressive forces bent on curtailing such progress.

With a relentless slew of tragedies and setbacks affecting Black Americans from all walks of life, these past few years are not likely to be a time that many Black people (or people of color in general) will look back on with undiluted pleasure. The wealth gap between the races (already significant) is growing wider. College is all but a distant wish for too many Black youths (and low-income youths of all races) as they are increasingly being priced out of higher education. Affirmative action is slowly chipped at by higher courts and is being treated in a passive-aggressive manner by our current Supreme Court.

With the exception of pockets of the Latino communities (and there are rifts there as well), relationships with other races and ethnicities, including White Americans, seem to be based on political convenience by the group in question, as opposed to any sustained commitment to forge a genuine allegiance with the Black community. In the minds of many other ethnic groups, they have been colonized to view Black people as aberrations. People to be seen as "the other." Dark, derelict, dangerous, deceptive, perhaps even demonic.

Black Americans have been racialized, brutalized, sexualized, and largely despised. We have been labeled as individuals not to be trusted or worthy of any minimal degree of sympathy. As the nation becomes ever more multicultural and xenophobia becomes an even greater threat, this could change as people of color may realize that it is more advantageous to form an alliance with another group that is opposed to being manipulated by larger racist forces who are determined to keep diverse ethnic groups in a balkanized state of affairs through manipulative tactics and propaganda.

While some segments of Black America are faring relatively well, far too many other factions are living in a state of crisis that is just as unsettling as the state that their parents and grandparents lived in under the oppressive era of segregation. This is a situation that is unacceptable and must be addressed by Americans of all races, in particular Black leadership or a new generation of leaders, as well as a government that will be attentive to the precarious plight that is facing too many Black Americans.

It is because of such undeniable and brutal realities that many people — across racial lines — are uncomfortable discussing an issue that is an integral part of our society, yet we must, in fact, do so. It is a crucial topic that is not going to absolve itself from public discourse simply because there are too many people (including some people of color) who are afraid to confront the issue. Deflecting and denying the issue will not save us.

In these most unsettling times, we must embrace hope and courage as much as we tend to pursue intense rhetoric and solutions. We as Americans must be willing to embrace one another, look internally and challenge one another to strive for, and embrace our better angels. We must adopt a politics of collectivism as opposed to one of crass and reductive individualism. A diverse and pluralistic society like ours will demand nothing less from us.

While I don't envision that we will return to the era of a legal, pre-Jim Crow America, the fact is that all of us who are committed to the cause of progress must make a valiant effort to ensure that such a regressive outcome will never reach fruition. To quote the late great, self-described Black, lesbian, feminist, warrior poet Audre Lorde "the war against dehumanization is ceaseless" (Lorde, 1984). Given the current, sordid state of affairs, such words are as relevant as ever.

REFERENCES

Barr, Andy (2009, February 18). Holder "Nation of cowards on race." *Politico*. Retrieved from https://www.politico.com/story/2009/02/holder-nation-of-cowards-on-race-018999

Lorde, Audre (1984). *Sister outsider: Essays and speeches by Audre Lorde*. Boston, MA: South End Press.

Mark, Michelle (2018, June 27). Justice Kennedy announces retirement, setting Trump up to reshape the Supreme Court for years to come. *Business Insider*. Retrieved from https://www.businessinsider.com.au/justice-kennedy-retires-supreme-court-2018-6

New York Times Editorial Board. There's so much you don't know about Brett Kavanaugh: And you probably won't until it's too late. *New York Times*. Retrieved from https://www.nytimes.com/2018/07/09/opinion/editorials/trump-kavanaugh-supreme-court-senate.html

Roe v. Wade, 410 U.S. (1973).

Shear, Michael (2018, June 27). Supreme Court Justice Anthony Kennedy will retire. *New York Times*. Retrieved from https://www.nytimes.com/2018/06/27/us/politics/anthony-kennedy-retire-supreme-court.html

Index